LIVING MUSIC IN SCHOOLS 1923-1999

For Sheila, Eustacia and Brendan

Living Music in Schools 1923-1999

Studies in the history of music education in England

GORDON COX
University of Reading, UK

Ashgate

Published by
Ashgate Publishing Limited
Gower House
Croft Road
Aldershot
Hampshire GU11 3HR
England

Ashgate Publishing Company
131 Main Street
Burlington, VT 05401-5600 USA

Ashgate website: http://www.ashgate.com

British Library Cataloguing in Publication Data
Cox, Gordon S. A.
Living music in schools 1923-1999 : studies in the history of music education in England
1. Music - Instruction and study - England - History - 20th century 2. Education - England - History - 20th century
I. Title
780.7'1'042'09049

Library of Congress Control Number: 2001099659

ISBN 0 7546 0631 7

Printed and bound in Great Britian by
Antony Rowe Ltd, Chippenham, Wiltshire

Contents

Acknowledgements

The labour of this book has been lightened by the interest and concern of friends and colleagues. First of all, thanks are due to those who took the trouble to read and comment on various drafts of chapters including Nicholas Bannan, Kevin Brehony, Helen Coll, Brendan Cox, Jack Dobbs, Anthony Kemp, John Paynter, Hamish Preston, Fraser Smith and Geoff Southworth. I am indebted to Vic Gammon from the University of Leeds for his insights and detailed recommendations stemming from his close and critical reading of the whole manuscript, and also for his comradely encouragement over the years.

I would like to thank those who organised and participated in the following symposia and meetings of professional associations for the opportunities to try out my ideas, and to clarify and extend them through dialogue: American Educational Research Association (San Diego, 1998), Canadian History of Education Society (University of British Columbia, 1998), the History of Education Seminars (Institute for Historical Research, London, 1997), the Research Commission of the International Society for Music Education (Magaliesberg and Pretoria, South Africa, 1998, and the University of Utah, 2000), the International Research in Music Education conference (University of Exeter, 1999), the Symposium in Tribute to Allen P. Britton (University of Maryland, College Park, 2000), and the Society for Research in Psychology of Music and Music Education (University of Cambridge, 1996). I would also like to acknowledge the support of Charles Plummeridge, particularly for his initiative in setting up a regular series of seminars on Studies in the History of Music Education at the Institute of Education, University of London, which have enabled like-minded researchers to meet on an annual basis to report on work in progress.

The libraries and archives which have provided me with helpful leads and documents include: the Bodleian Library, Oxford; the BBC Written Archives, Caversham; the EMI Music Archives, Hayes; the Music Education History Archive, University of Reading; the National Sound Archive, London; the Public Record Office, Kew.

Thanks are also due to the late Arnold Bentley for several illuminating conversations concerning his own part in the development of music education particularly in the Schools Council years, and to the late Bernarr Rainbow who shared generously of his vast knowledge of music education history.

A particular privilege has been to record interviews with teachers and past students in the Reading University/Schools Partnership PGCE Course. I am grateful for their forbearance and also for their generosity in relating to me their own experiences. Also to Katy Lyne and Helen Thompson for their transcribing skills. This part of the research has been supported by a grant from the University of Reading Research Endowment Trust Fund. I also received a small grant towards preparing the book for publication from the University of Reading School of Education.

During the final stage of the book's completion I have received invaluable help in the preparation of the manuscript from Brian Peters, and technical support from Brian Evans, whilst Caroline Cornish and Rachel Lynch from Ashgate have been encouraging and supportive editors.

For my wife Sheila, and children, Eustacia and Brendan, to whom this book is dedicated, I would like to express my gratitude for the crucial support they have provided me, each in their own inimitable way.

Versions of Chapters 2 through 6, and the Afterword have appeared elsewhere, and I am grateful to publishers and editors for permission to draw upon these papers as indicated: Chapters 1 and 7, and the material in Chapter 6 concerning student music teachers appear here for the first time.

'Music in Schools, 1923-1999: an educational debate' is a much expanded and revised version of 'Music in Schools 1923-1999: some historical reflections', in C. Plummeridge and C. Philpott, eds, *Issues in Music Teaching* (London: Routledge/Falmer 2001), pp. 9-20. Permission granted by Routledge/Falmer.

'Changing the Face of School Music: Walford Davies and the Development of BBC School Music Broadcasts 1924-1947' combines and revises the following: 'Changing the Face of School Music: Walford Davies, the Gramophone and the Radio', *British Journal of Music Education* 14 (1997), 45-55; 'School Music Broadcasts and the BBC 1924-47', *History of Education* 25 (1996), 363-71. Permission granted respectively by Cambridge University Press, and Taylor and Francis.

'Musical Education of the Under-Twelves 1949-1983' is an expanded version of 'Musical Education of the Under-Twelves (MEUT) 1949-1983: Some Aspects of the History of Post-war Primary Music Education', *British Journal of Music Education* 15 (1998), 239-53. Permission granted by Cambridge University Press.

'A House Divided: Music Education during the Schools Council Era of the 1970s' is an expanded and revised version of 'A House Divided: Music Education in the United Kingdom during the Schools Council Era of the 1970s', *Journal of Historical Research in Music Education* XXII (2001), 160-75. Permission from Arizona State University, granted by the editors, Jere Humphreys and George Heller.

'Talking about Music Teaching: Recollections and Realities' is a reconceived and much expanded version of 'Secondary School Music Teachers Talking', *Music Education Research* 1 (1999), 37-45. Permission granted by Taylor and Francis.

'Towards a Usable Past for Music Educators' is a revised version of 'Towards a Usable Past for Music Educators', *History of Education* 28 (1999), 449-58. Permission granted by Taylor and Francis.

1 Introduction

We are experiencing a musical revolution. Electronic culture and its immense potentialities are transforming the ways we create, consume and participate in music. We are at a crossroads. The temptation for music educators is to jettison traditional practice, and join the seemingly inevitable onward march of progress without too much reflection. But the progress of music education is not inevitable, nor is it predictable. Indeed like the history of education, music education history is 'a contested and changing terrain' (Aldrich, 2000, 63). The purpose of this book is to provide a window on the past, so that we can place current developments both within the historical landscape of music education, and within the processes of contest and change in the school curriculum.

In my previous book, *A History of Music Education in England 1872-1928* (Cox, 1993), I presented a view of music education mediated through the work of Her/His Majesty's Inspectorate of Schools (HMI). It inevitably reflected the formulation of policy, and the motivations and philosophies of key individuals within the educational establishment. In this present work I explore more recent history and cast my net wider, in order to investigate a richer variety of musical and educational experiences so as to understand more clearly the complex relationship between rhetoric and practice.

Although the book preserves a roughly chronological treatment, there has been no attempt to write a complete history of music education. It is the emphasis upon the lived experiences of making music in schools that provides the key to the stance I have taken, which is also implicit in the book's title. I wanted to reconstruct not only the process of policy making, but the reception of innovative ideas within classrooms by teachers whose professional lives have embraced a bewildering myriad of educational reforms. I deal, therefore, with reforms which aimed to breathe life into music in schools, and at the same time describe what it was like for music teachers whose professional lives were dedicated to living the subject in schools.

Music's location in the school curriculum has been bitterly contested over the years. For example, in 1873 John Curwen wrote a pamphlet entitled *The Present Crisis of Music in Schools* two years after music had been omitted from the Educational Code, whilst in the 1990s in the context of the National Curriculum, Malcolm Ross made a blistering attack asking 'What's wrong with School Music?' 1.6 (1995). In his recent book *Teaching Music Musically* (1999), Keith Swanwick has pointed out the long history of negative attitudes to school music on the part of pupils, particularly those in secondary schools.

1

Tellingly he contrasts the positive attitudes of student teachers when they start to develop their teaching, with their experience two or three years later 'when the shine has rubbed off and the system has ground their energy away' (ibid., 102). To continue with Swanwick's thinking, on the one hand we know that genuine musical experience has within it something of metaphorical richness containing several layers of meaning, but how can one teacher and every single school hope to encompass it? Can we guarantee that pupils receive a musically authentic experience (using and encountering 'real' instruments, 'real' music, 'real' musicians, and 'real' music-making settings)? These questions, and a search for some often elusive answers underlie my historical treatment.

Behind these concerns about relating policy to practice, and influencing the effectiveness of music teaching, lies the intention to press for a serious recognition of music education history within the parent discipline of the history of education. At a Music Educators National Conference in Washington DC in March 2000, the distinguished American educational historian Barbara Finkelstein attempted to answer the question 'what might happen if music education was treated as an important concern in the history of education?' Her answers were encouraging. Such a stance might break down the balkanisation of the history of education, because music occupies a space that educational historians have not entered. As music sits inside a culture, it can reveal the processes of cultural transmission, whether referring to young people, immigrants, women, or to the 'invisible realities' of homes and communities. Through an investigation of this space we might understand better the nature of cultural transmission.

Through drawing attention to the potential richness of the history of music education, and its ability to reveal music's unique space within cultures, I hope that the book may encourage music teachers to explore aspects of their collective past, to renew their attempts to inculcate a passion for music amongst the pupils they teach, and hence to revitalise their own working lives.

Now for some detailed description of the book's contents. In each chapter I incorporate a broad range of views which range from educational rhetoric to classroom reality. Themes of the potential of music in education, institutional constraints and the experience of teaching music are interwoven throughout.

Chapter 2 provides an overall view of the period under discussion: 1923-1999. It does this in order to orientate the reader, and to contextualise the rest of the book. Both dates precede two significant developments in music education: the commencement of school music broadcasts by the BBC in 1924, and the introduction of a new version of the National Curriculum in 2000. The chapter is based upon 'snapshots' of the music education press taken at 25-year intervals, and deals with new ideas, their implementation and teacher concerns. Thus the stage is set for the historical case studies which are presented in the next four chapters: they comprise the heart of the book.

Chapter 3 focuses on the development of BBC school music broadcasts between 1924 and 1947 which were an outcome of the Corporation's educational remit. They offered an opportunity for music teachers to expand the scope of music in schools, and to transform it. Hence the chapter looks at music education through the lens of an organisation whose aims were not as institutionally confined or restricted as those of schools: as a result there was the potential to extend the boundaries of what was possible. In particular the chapter investigates the work of Walford Davies (one of the most popular broadcasters of the time), and his belief in the potential of the new media to change the face of school music. I examine his attempts to develop tune building as an important part of children's musical experience, and I assess the reasons for the eventual collapse of the project. I contrast Davies's broadcasts with the very different approaches of Ann Driver in *Music and Movement*, and Herbert Wiseman in *Singing Together*.

Chapter 4 is a study of the post-war development of music in primary schools through the work of a music teachers' association, Musical Education of the Under-Twelves (MEUT). Here, in contrast to the BBC, was a grass roots movement, stemming from the teacher training colleges. At the same time it also represented such pre-war interest groups as the Percussion Band Association, the Pipers' Guild, and the Bow-Craft Guild. Its founding members, mostly women, were committed to an overall progressive educational stance, encouraging a child-centred approach to music teaching. I trace the development of such thinking within the association from its birth in 1949 until its demise in 1984. Hand in hand with these developments, however, were persistent worries about how so-called 'creative' approaches could be married with traditional concerns, such as the teaching of music reading and musical literacy. The association's heyday was in the 1960s. In the following decade it found itself out of step with the more astringent times.

Chapter 5 addresses the musical implications of the work of the Schools Council, possibly the most important post-war curriculum development body in the United Kingdom. Its two major music projects came to symbolise in the 1970s what Swanwick called 'a house divided'. The chapter looks in detail at the two projects, 'Music Education of Young Children' directed by Arnold Bentley, and 'Music in the Secondary School Curriculum' directed by John Paynter. They represented the two extremes of a divide within music education, emphasising respectively musical literacy and musical creativity. The chapter explores the tension between the two projects. It also focuses on the wider remit of the Schools Council Music Committee, in particular its somewhat defensive reactions to proposals to broaden the scope of music education through the development of projects concerned with the integration of the arts in the curriculum.

Chapter 6 provides the final case study, based upon the opinions and beliefs of 20 music teachers and student music teachers. It sets out to discover what their experiences of being taught music were like, reasons for deciding to make music teaching a career, and the realities of their working lives. A central theme is their response to innovations. What is presented is a collective biography, in which the concerns of practising teachers are paramount. The chapter concludes that we need to think radically about the future, and be ready to re-define roles in order to generate fresh ways of working.

Chapter 7 looks at the future of music education in the light of the preceding studies. It asks what lessons we can learn from a consideration of the case studies, in particular about the continuing struggle to establish a place for music as a school subject, and the process of curriculum change and its relationship with classroom realities and music teachers. It considers some of the implications for music educators of the current musical revolution, and outlines research possibilities that might help enhance the whole process of living music in schools.

Finally, in the Afterword, I present some thoughts about the history of music education, and about new possibilities which researchers might want to investigate. Its title, 'Towards a Usable Past for Music Educators', indicates the drift of my thinking. First it presents a critique of the work of Bernarr Rainbow with its celebration of a rose-tinted past which resulted in a disengagement with contemporary culture. My argument is that if we are to reform music education we need a broader definition of what it is. In particular, the Afterword reviews work that has been carried out which relates to four themes: localised studies of music instruction; images of music teachers; pedagogical texts; and music education, class and culture. Such a broadening of horizons to encompass formal and informal experiences of music education may help to liberate us from our institutionalised view. The theme that permeates the discussion, however, is the possibility of developing a usable past for music educators; one which establishes dynamic connections between the past, present and future.

I believe the book is needed for three reasons. First, it presents new information about such major developments in the history of music education as the BBC School Music Broadcasts and the Schools Council's music projects. Second, it details music teacher responses to the musical changes in schools, and charts the details of the often heated debates involving teachers which took place in associations, committees, and in the press. Third, its emphasis upon bridging the divide between curriculum rhetoric and classroom realities, represents an advance within the historiography of music education.

As for methodology, I have found that the toolkit necessary for studying curriculum history necessitates a variety of strategies. In my research for this book I have worked with numerous documents and artefacts: in archives seeking out primary data concerning the BBC, the Schools Council, and Musical Education of the Under-Twelves, in libraries reading music teacher periodicals, and in school music rooms interviewing and tape recording teachers and student teachers. This range of methods from the life histories of individual teachers to the history of music as a school subject is crucial, in order to catch some of the richness of the curriculum with its influence on resources, school finance, teacher status and career structures.

The work is based upon seven previously published essays, together with new material arising from tape-recorded conversations with student music teachers. However, all these essays have been substantially revised and expanded in order to develop the arguments that I have been debating throughout the last seven years concerning the place of music in the school curriculum, and the relationship of all this to the history of education.

2 Music in Schools 1923-1999: An Educational Debate

The purpose of this chapter is to provide an overview of the period under discussion. This will set the scene for the subsequent historical case studies.

During 1998 and 1999 there was a furious debate about the perceived threat to the teaching of music in schools. It was chronicled by *The Times Educational Supplement* (*TES*), which also sponsored a fighting campaign 'Music for the Millennium'. This crisis prompted me to chart historically the continuities and discontinuities in the teaching of music in schools in order to understand more clearly the shifting alliances and struggles which have characterised the process of music 'becoming a subject' (see Goodson, 1994). Through reading the *TES* columns relating to the debate concerning 'Music for the Millennium', I identified three main questions that I wanted to pursue historically with the intention of discerning some underlying patterns: how have the aims and justifications for the teaching of music changed and developed? What have been the principal innovations in the music curriculum over the years? How have music teachers responded to these innovations in their teaching? In order to trace these issues I read a selection of music education professional journals at four 25-year intervals, commencing in 1923-1924, until 1998-1999. Such journals might be taken to be representative of music teachers' reading. They included the *School Music Review* (1923-1925), *Music Teacher* (1923-1924, 1948-1949, 1973-1974, 1998-1999), *Music in Education* (1947-1950, 1973-1974), and *The Times Educational Supplement* (1998-1999).

I shall discuss the three main questions through snapshots taken at these four 25-year intervals and shall precede each of the four sections with a brief contextual introduction. In comparing the accounts no doubt at times my chosen themes will elide: at other times they will collide.

1. 1923-1924

We need to recollect the general context of the early 1920s. Politically, in the election of 1922 the Conservatives had a clear majority and a year later Stanley Baldwin took over from Bonar Law. In 1924 with Liberal assistance and backing, the first Labour government took office headed by Ramsay MacDonald. Educationally, by 1919 the elementary school system had been firmly established for nearly half a century. Since the 1902 Education Act a system of secondary schools had been built up, but even by 1920 only one in ten elementary school children proceeded to them (Simon, 1974). Education policy was subject to strict economy. Between October 1922 and January 1923 Conservative governments placed a greater priority on the construction of houses than on the building of schools. The year 1923 was notable for lengthy and bitter teachers' strikes, as some local authorities sought to pay lower salaries than those determined by Burnham, and to employ unqualified staff (see Gordon, Aldrich, Dean, 1991).

The justifications for the teaching of music during these years ranged from the idealist to the pragmatic. We read of a high-minded view in a critique (*School Music Review*, July 1923) of a book entitled *Spirit and Music* written by Hunt (1922). Hunt believed that music needed to be valued as a subject, not merely as a part of life, a means of earning a living or of relaxation, but also more importantly as 'a manifestation of the divine spirit' (ibid., 51). Music in schools, particularly folk tunes and dances, could provide an outlet for the emotions, and stimulate imaginative play. Consequently it could be socially regenerative:

> the prosaic life and surroundings of the slum child are sufficiently deadening and the new mental picture this gives are in the nature of windows opening on new vistas of life. They suggest views that could come to the child's mind in no other ways. (*School Music Review*, July 1923, 97)

This rhetoric contrasts with the more down-to-earth advice given to music teachers as regards classroom principles. The official guide to music teaching up until the end of the Second World War lay in the continually revised *Handbook of Suggestions for Teachers*. The *School Music Review* (December 1923) welcomed the new edition of 1923, noting that the chapter on 'Singing' (as the subject was called) was a reprint of the 1914 version. Nevertheless it repaid reading again because of its sound general principles and the freedom it allowed teachers within these principles. The principles were encompassed through the teaching of songs, voice training, ear training and sight reading.

Walter Carroll, the music adviser of Manchester, filled in some detail (*School Music Review*, February 1924). He outlined eight aims for elementary schoolchildren up to 14. These included the cultivation of: a love of music for its own sake; good breathing habits; a sweet voice with forward tone and no breaks or registers; a sensitive ear for pitch and rhythm; a facility in reading simple tunes from staff notation; a large number of good songs; an appreciation of music through rhythm, melody and harmony; and knowledge of music literature through hearing standard works performed well.

Rhetoric and practice in the sense of a broadening of horizons did come closer together in some of the curriculum innovations of these years particularly in tune building, musical appreciation, and concerts for children.

A recently released set of gramophone records made by Walford Davies for HMV, entitled *Melody Lectures*, was advertised in the January 1923 issue of *Music Teacher*. One of these records contained examples of tunes composed by children. Davies was convinced the majority of children could be tune-builders (*Music Teacher*, January 1923) but he observed that remarkably few children in schools were taught the simple rules of the game of melody, although he emphasised that like any game it was not enough to be merely taught in books and classrooms. Whilst one-third of a music course might be found in instruction books, the most exciting two-thirds should be spent in the activity of making music. All this led him to outline a detailed plan: the whole school should meet for a daily sing for ten minutes, learning fifty melodies a term, and then the boys would learn to construct their own tunes. Davies believed in the simple truth that 'melody is our real mother-tongue', and consequently the tune building of the pupils may enable them to inhabit 'the little creative heaven of sound' (ibid., 194). Davies was to preach this gospel not only through the gramophone, but increasingly through the wireless: in 1924 he presented the first schools broadcast on the BBC.

Perhaps the most significant innovation however was music appreciation. It was Carroll's opinion (*School Music Review*, February 1924) that school music needed both action (music by doing) and contemplation (listening), but in his opinion the latter received much less attention than the former. This observation was developed by Geoffrey Shaw (HMI):

> children ... so rarely listen; they are always performing ... There is no possible basis for the study of musical form and literature as a school subject, except through ear training, familiarity with notation, and an extremely good grounding in good song literature. Appreciation is the correlating of musical experiences. (*School Music Review*, March 1924, 269)

Shaw's observation placed 'appreciation' within the tradition already established by the *Handbook of Suggestions*, with the emphasis upon the teaching of songs, voice training, ear training and sight reading. But we also sense a concern in Shaw's comments that 'appreciation' might be seen as something separate.

However, the apostle of the new movement, Stewart MacPherson, was anxious to preserve the distinctiveness of Musical Appreciation. He believed that as any cause becomes popular there is usually danger ahead. In an article for *Music Teacher* (January 1923) he clearly set out the problem: he welcomed the fact that the new movement had 'caught on', but like all new movements it also suffered from 'the zeal untempered by discretion of not a few of its supporters' (ibid., 203). Consequently, MacPherson argued, the teaching of Musical Appreciation should certainly not be the province of every teacher.

Much of the teaching associated with 'appreciation' was in his opinion profoundly bad. He outlined the essential qualities that were needed for the effective teaching of musical appreciation: the teacher needed enthusiasm ('it is impossible to kindle a fire from an icicle' [ibid.]), but above all a deep appreciation and grasp of the art of music itself. Whilst the primary school teacher might deal with the rudimentary stages of class singing and ear training well

> beyond that ... he cannot go; the waters are too deep, and the subtleties and complexities of an art had better be left to those whose life has been given to their unravelling. (Ibid., 204)

MacPherson's recommendation was that specialised teachers should be employed whose duty should be to visit in turn all the schools in given areas teaching Appreciation lessons.

The third development during these years was related to musical appreciation, and provided an expansion of opportunities for children to hear music outside the school. On 29 March 1924, the inaugural concert for children promoted by Robert Mayer was presented at Westminster Central Hall (*School Music Review*, May 1924):

> In spite of strike difficulties some 1500 children were present. ... Mr Mayer had in mind the children's concerts conducted by Mr Walter Damrosch in the United States and desires to arrange a series along similar lines in London. (Ibid., 333)

This concert was conducted by Adrian Boult, whilst Damrosch was to conduct the next programme on 17 May, which included Weber's overture, Oberon, the Andante from Haydn's Surprise Symphony, the allegretto from Beethoven's 8th Symphony, the Rakowsky March of Berlioz, and the Beautiful Blue Danube Waltz. In the review of this concert (*School Music Review*, June 1924) the critic exclaimed

> what a marvellous force is personality! ... Musicians sometimes take music so seriously and heavily that children feel crushed beneath the weight ... This was not the case on May 17th.

The movement gained momentum fast. Manchester City Council approved a series of municipal orchestral concerts with 500 seats reserved for elementary and secondary school pupils, whilst official recognition had been given children's concerts by the Board of Education, with the proviso that local education authorities had to provide the money. The London County Council was to allow children to attend musical lectures in school time (see *School Music Review*, December 1924).

Such innovations during these years helped to develop creative music making, and to reinforce the momentum of musical appreciation, and presumably its effectiveness in allowing masses of children the opportunity to listen to music played by professionals on the gramophone and wireless, and in real life.

But the conditions for implementing these new ideas in schools were not ideal. In an article on 'Appreciation in an Elementary School', E.R. Lewis (*Music Teacher*, August 1924) informs us that of the three classes in his school, two numbered 65 pupils each, whilst the third had 40 pupils. Each group was assigned two half-hour periods weekly for music. Much of the time was taken up with vocal training in Tonic Sol-fa and staff notations. This work was regarded as difficult by both teachers and pupils. The subject was taught by two members of the ordinary school staff. Appreciation was a welcome innovation, but it had to be approached circumspectly. At first it comprised one in six lessons, and later was extended to include a short piece of pianoforte music played three days a week to the whole school assembly, whilst on a fourth morning a gramophone record was played.

There were however more highly favoured schools which blazed the trail of musical excellence. One of the key centres for developing the music curriculum was Mary Datchelor's School in Camberwell, London, the subject of one of the Board of Education's pamphlets (*School Music Review*, June 1923). A special grant had been awarded the school from 1919, which provided for a two-year course of further study for those girls who having reached the standard for the General School Certificate Examination, demonstrated that they possessed special musical ability. In this further course of study, between 20 and 30 periods per week were spent by these musically able girls in music. Eventually most of them took up music professionally, and some entered teaching.

The school laid the foundation of this advanced course early on in the curriculum. In a demonstration of the work of the school to the Music Teachers' Association (*Music Teacher*, January 1923), what is noteworthy is the focus upon composition and improvisation. Two pieces were composed specially by the Advanced Course music students for the kindergarten percussion band. The 10-12 year olds demonstrated vocal improvisation, improvising a folk song on a given pattern. In the middle school a pupil played her own piano sonata. This was a scheme which provided hope for the future, and enhanced the status of the subject.

Questions of status, professionalism and training were in the forefront of music teachers' concerns at this time. Proper training was one of the keys to enhanced professionalism. There was a need for a new diploma (*School Music Review*, June 1923) which would ensure that teachers who otherwise had had little musical experience, apart from that gained in training college, could improve themselves. The School Music Teacher's Certificate organised by the Tonic Sol-fa College was reckoned to be too narrow, too tied to a text book. A glance at the contents of the official textbooks reveals an exhaustive but rather mechanical approach to sight singing, musical dictation, time and staff notation, and musical theory (see Evans and McNaught, 1903, and Venables, n.d.). Their thinking reflects the late nineteenth-century priority of teaching sight singing *en masse* in schools. The certificate was clearly becoming out of step with the times.

Suggestions for change included the possibility that perhaps local education authorities (LEAs) could increase the musical scope of qualifications: why not an LCC (London County Council) Diploma of Music? The dilemma was that the LRAM was too difficult. A relevant diploma needed to cover ear training, sight singing, rhythmic movement, musical appreciation, history, musical form and harmony. The *School Music Review* (July 1923) reported the following month that the Tonic Sol-fa College had set up a special committee 'instituting a new diploma for school teachers whose needs will be specially remembered in the light of modern developments in school methods' (ibid., 29-30).

The overriding impression received from these years is of the growing possibilities that were becoming available. The New Year editorial in *School Music Review* (January 1925) encapsulates this:

> 1924 has seen the inception of wireless talks for schools ... Another landmark is the inclusion of Music as a subject for matriculation ... Some of London's children will have the privilege in the near future of attending, in school terms, a course of lectures with musical illustrations on a larger scale than is possible in school ... and what of 1925? Teachers are becoming breathless with the effort of trying to keep up with the swift movement of events. No longer is there need for them to pine for more musical opportunities ... preparation should be the watchword of the music teacher and the general teacher who takes music. With increased opportunities the child will learn much about music and will want to know still more. (Ibid., 225)

Whilst music in schools was still based largely upon the vocally based curriculum (indeed the subject was called 'Singing' in elementary schools until 1927), which provided its own skills-based teaching, there was a movement towards a more reflective stance based upon 'appreciation', as well as a view of music which might encompass feelings and imagination through melody making. The twin developments of the gramophone and the children's concerts had the potential to engage large numbers of children with the professional world of music making. But there was also some work in secondary schools which catered for more academic perspectives and strengthened the academic tradition within the subject. Finally, the material interests of teachers were interlinked with the fate of their subject specialism.

They wanted professional status, and the training relevant to new developments.

2. 1947-1948

The immediate post-war years were full of difficulties for the Labour government: a crisis in coal production through an exceptionally freezing winter and a serious financial crisis when the country faced bankruptcy, while still recovering from the war effort. Educationally 1947 saw the school-leaving age finally raised to fifteen, and a report recommending the replacement of the School Certificate by the General Certificate of Education. The government was also determined to implement the 1944 Education Act and to impose a tripartite solution on the country's secondary sector, with the development of grammar, technical and modern schools (see Simon, 1991).

The Act was followed by a stream of publications, and the alphabetical slogans which encapsulated the changes: Age, Ability and Aptitude. In an article entitled 'Music Education since the 1944 Education Act', Percy Smith (*Music in Education*, January-February 1950) pointed out that the events of the war had broken the apathetic appreciation of music, into which the country had so comfortably settled. This meant that music witnessed an extraordinary revival of interest, and presumably this influenced the framers of the Act in which wide powers were given to all those who studied and practised music. After all, Smith continued, no other subject is so complete in the range of demands placed on those who study it. The most significant change had come about through the universities where music had been accorded a regular place as a matriculation and School Certificate subject, as well as providing arts courses in which music was a main subject. It was envisaged that eventually there would be music specialists in all junior and secondary schools. Present shortages were being filled by the government's Emergency Training Scheme: one of the most urgent matters was to provide, as quickly as possible, good music teachers for the schools.

In a speech to the Schools' Music Association (*Music in Education*, March-April 1947) Cyril Winn (HMI) considered the implications of the proposed leaving age of 15, and his last phrase reflects a longstanding controversy about whether or not music should be compulsory for all pupils:

> He stressed the need for encouraging boys and girls to develop their appreciation for good music, while he agreed that those who showed little or no interest in music should concentrate on those cultural subjects in which their aptitudes lay. (Ibid., 28)

With reference to the School Certificate, Crabtree (*Music in Education*, March-

April 1947) pointed out that the McNair Report had urged a full-scale musical offensive on the schools, so much so that many schools could now boast about music being part of the regular curriculum. But few schools treated music as a full class subject right up to the School Certificate. It was, however, important to Crabtree 'to deal with the subject as a class subject spread over a number of years' (ibid., 12). The vast majority of pupils would be able to cope with at least the early stages. This might help to increase the take-up of the subject, and improve the current situation which music shared with Urdu and spinning, of only having one examiner each at School Certificate level.

It was apparent that instrumental teaching was becoming a priority. It presaged a new form of musical provision in schools:

> Music in schools has in the past been mainly devoted to singing, and instrumental music has only flourished in schools with special facilities where private teachers have been engaged to teach individual children ... By teaching these instruments in classes, the school orchestra, instead of being quite beyond the means of many schools, may now become formally established in most secondary schools. (*Music in Education*, March-April 1947, 27)

In a later issue we read that the Reading Youth Committee in 1942 had spent a substantial amount of money on orchestral instruments, and had inaugurated schemes for young people to loan and have an instrument for 6d. per lesson. This had led to the present Reading Youth Orchestra having 45 members (*Music in Education*, July-August 1947).

Through a somewhat partial comparison by Gordon Hendricks between secondary school music in America and Great Britain, it is possible to grasp some overall trends (*Music in Education*, July-August 1949). Hendricks is worth quoting at length:

> In America it seems we generally give our little girls a baton, tap shoes and a costume of white satin and ask them to act like Shirley Temple. In England, children of the same age are given a recorder and taught to play folk tunes. In America we give our little boys a cornet - preferably a gold one in a purple plush case, and a gold-braided uniform - and ask them to play such delights as 'Thoughts of Gold', 'Bride of the Waves', and 'Whispering Hope'. In England at the same age, they are usually singing good music better than the average American adult ... In England at least two-fifths of all school children regularly listen to broadcasts of great music beamed directly to their school rooms. (Ibid., 70)

Hendricks points to the too-close association in the USA between band directors and instrumental manufacturers, which because of the narrow focus upon instrumentation and repertoire, prevented the public from encountering the great masterpieces of music. Apparently in Great Britain there was less of a problem, because stringed instruments predominated, and wind instruments were too expensive.

During these post-war years there were some music educators who attempted a fundamental reassessment of music teaching. For example, A.H. Radcliffe in an article entitled significantly 'Education through Music' (*Music in Education*, January-February 1948) expressed concern about the institutionalisation of music:

> while school education is handled as a thing apart, as it all too often is, while it is undertaken in a social vacuum, it can strike children only as unreal and completely non-vital. (Ibid., 165)

If education was a process, rather than merely having content, it followed that a music teacher's concepts of education were at least as important as his musical capacities. The problem with music was that its objectives in schools were ill-defined and ill-considered: we had lost sight of education in our concentration on pure technique.

In some ways this theme was developed by one of the pioneers of the Percussion Band movement, Louie de Rusette. She believed in the importance of the present moment. The child should be encouraged to express himself through rhythm, melody and harmony (*Music in Education*, May-June 1948). Mere imitation killed initiative, forestalled nature and dwarfed the personality. She asked: why should music be different from art in schools? Children were encouraged to paint and draw according to their present powers of observation and experience. Too often in schools children were penalised because they were not felt ready to produce accurate sounds. On the contrary de Rusette declared: 'We shall not become a musical nation until music is treated as a creative art in the Primary school.'

If such views were growing they were still not generally representative of the majority. J.H. White (*Music in Education*, September-October 1947) addressed what he regarded as the fundamentals. By the time most children left school at the age of 15 three main aims should have been achieved musically: interest aroused and stimulated; the child would know the best use of the voice; and a simple line of staff notation would be able to be read. Admittedly White thought these aims modest in scope, but asked rhetorically: how many schools realise them? There were clearly manifold musical activities in schools: choir, percussion band, recorder playing, eurhythmics, festivals, instrumental tuition, and use of gramophone and wireless. But it was important they did not obscure the fundamentals. Although appreciation was not included in this list, White thought it should permeate musical experience whilst at school:

We should never lose sight of the fact that the first duty of the school is to provide a musically intelligent public, not to train executants. (Ibid., 101)

The main priority remained musical literacy for White. And yet he found the reading of staff notation neglected in schools. He recommended Tonic Sol-fa as an approach:

During twenty years of teaching, I cheerfully admit that I have never taught Staff Notation without using Tonic Sol-fa as a stepping stone. Without its help, the difficulties would appal me ... Generally where Tonic Sol-fa is taught, sight-reading is taught. (Ibid.)

But White accused his music educationist colleagues of pulling hard in different directions. There was so much talk, and so little achievement:

I have even heard of Inspectors who counsel the young music teacher to give up teaching classical songs and substitute the latest song hits! ... Some would turn all children into little pianists, others into little violinists. Some again would send them all, prepared or unprepared, to hear full orchestral concerts. This latter does good to some of the children, but in London at least it has proved ruination to the upholstery ... So much money and well-meaning effort is expended now, and so little, relatively, is achieved. (Ibid.)

Reginald Hunt (*Music Teacher*, June 1948) listed the four essential aims of school music teaching: to ensure musical literacy; to afford practical experience of music and music-making; to promote a knowledge of and liking for the best music; and ultimately to bring about a cultivated and urbane outlook on life, as a result of musical training. He elaborated on these points. He believed that 'musical illiteracy should call forth the same condemnation of an educational system as illiteracy in its more common sense' (ibid., 218). Essentially passivity is foreign to a music class, music education was justified through the actual performance of music. Listening to music apparently appealed to adolescent boys, and the increased emphasis upon it in schools appeared to have been one of the causes of increased attendance at concerts. Finally, in Hunt's eyes, music was able to appeal to the better natures of young people, and effect a refining influence upon them.

In schools, instrumental teaching was clearly in the ascendant, whether of orchestral instruments or the class percussion band. R.J. Snell wrote a series of articles on Music Teaching in Schools for *Music Teacher* in 1948. Whilst sight reading still played an essential role in the scheme of things, he maintained it could be taught more effectively using the whole range of instrumental resources available to a teacher: percussion bands, string classes, the recorder, and bamboo pipes. He devoted one article to the percussion band as an effective teaching tool. Through it children were able to experience at first hand the making of music. Moreover, through participation in such a musical activity, pupils developed the powers of concentration, team work and leadership. But more than this, percussion bands were a means of expression, developing the power of listening, providing broad ideas of musical colour, rhythm, pulse, accent and form (see *Music Teacher*, May 1948).

Reginald Hunt (*Music Teacher*, June 1948) concurred. He maintained that instruments provided a great deal of value in the teaching of musical literacy, and pointed to the piano class as perhaps the most practical method. After all, he argued, the keyboard was a more tangible and precise aid in this respect than the voice.

Area and youth orchestras began to represent unrivalled opportunities for children to take part in music. The National Youth Orchestra made its first appearance in 1948 (*Music Teacher*, June 1948), whilst at a more local level Elizabeth Lumb wrote about her secondary modern school brass band in Bradford, which within four years had gained fourth place in the relevant section of the National Championships (*Music Teacher*, September 1949).

The link between orchestras and 'musical appreciation' had been considerably strengthened in 1946, the year in which the Crown Film Unit produced a film called *Instruments of the Orchestra*, specifically for use in the classroom (*School Music Review*, March-April 1947). Composed by Benjamin Britten, and conducted by Malcolm Sargent with the London Symphony Orchestra, it was directed by Muir Mathieson. Mathieson was enthusiastic about the potential of film for delivering an effective music education. He had been closely associated with Richard Addinsell's *Warsaw Concerto* in *Dangerous Moonlight*, and wondered 'how many people listened to their first full concerto as a result of the Warsaw? I know quite a few' (ibid., 39).

He extended his love of film, to the context of cinemas, where he was conducting a series of children's morning symphony concerts in Middlesex:

> Children have the opportunity, in their own town, to hear good music under favourable conditions in surroundings that are familiar and congenial to them ... In many respects the cinema can assist the cause of music education if we make up our mind to sweep away old-fashioned prejudices, accept the cinema as a vital part of our daily lives, deplore that which is bad, encourage that which is good, and strive to ensure that the fullest possible use be made of this vast potential source of education and instruction. (Ibid., 40)

Film, like the children's orchestral concerts of the 1920s, and the gramophone and wireless in music classrooms, had the potential to popularise and extend the boundaries of music education. Taking concerts into cinemas helped break down the isolation of music within schools that Radcliffe was concerned about.

A penetrating insight into teaching during these years was provided by Gordon Reynolds in an article entitled 'The Secondary School Music Master' (*Music Teacher*, June 1948). Reynolds had intended to be a church organist, but as a result of his work in the Forces found himself organising choral groups and music clubs. Consequently he took a school music diploma, and became the sole music master in a couple of schools. Every class, he tells us, was allocated 40 minutes per week, and the teaching extended from Tonic Sol-fa, to the School Certificate, the Higher School Certificate, and Scholarship work. Because of an overcrowded timetable, everything else, including choirs and orchestras, took place after school. His working day extended therefore until 5.30 p.m. and longer on a Friday. He bemoaned having to teach the ABC stage: pupils had little experience in primary school. But for Reynolds the greatest joy was the choral work: 'don't expect to grow rich or fat, but you would be dull indeed if you were not at least occasionally spiritually warmed by your endeavours' (ibid., 380). Following on this question of rewards, Reginald Hunt noted that although music teachers were responsible for the high profile corporate life of the school, it was rare for them to be given posts of responsibility (*Music Teacher*, October 1948).

During these years the issue of the training of music teachers was a preoccupation reflected in the columns of *Music in Education*. In an article on Shenstone Training College (*Music in Education*, May-June 1947) emphasis was placed on the implications for music teaching of the Emergency Training Scheme. Ample opportunity was afforded the teaching practice: 13 weeks in four terms, as above all the scheme had to demonstrate professional relevance, so that practical teaching was not an interruption but a naturally felt need. There was a realisation that music lessons had to take on a fresh perspective: 'the singing lesson of days gone by is certainly not to be perpetuated' (ibid., 43). The students' own musical abilities were recognised, but with an eye to the classroom and teaching methods. They gradually learned to deal with songs, ear training, sight reading, listening and appreciation work. But all this was not confined to schools. The male choir, instrumentalists and vocalists gave concerts in the local town hall: they had first-hand experience of non-competitive music festivals where they heard singing, percussion bands, pipe playing and recorders, verse speaking and massed singing.

All this rubbed off on the traditional training college course. Aries asked: 'why can't we evolve a system of teacher training which uses the emergency and older methods?' (*Music in Education*, September-October 1947). The most outstanding feature of the Emergency scheme appears to have been the recruitment of tutors with many years of varied teaching experience, who were able to demonstrate practically to their students. As a result their courses were more professionally relevant. The writer reckoned that students needed more than the GRSM (Graduate of the Royal Schools of Music) offered. Training should have three main targets: students trained in musicianship;

application of this to teaching; and a vision of the importance, place and implications of music in the everyday community of the school as a whole. To achieve this, the importation of more experienced school music teachers into the permanent teacher training colleges to work as tutors was necessary, so that courses would become practical, and relevant to nearly all the students.

A portrait of the Southern Music Training Centre in Ewell (*Music in Education*, November-December 1948) provides more detail of the variety of training procedures. The Centre's predecessor, the Surrey College of Music, had been opened in 1946 by Professor E.J. Dent, under the presidency of Sir Arnold Bax. Evening classes were introduced for already qualified teachers, and in the daytime children were trained in elementary musicianship leading to the School Certificate, so that adult students would be able to observe class methods and practice on the classes. A year later the college was approached by the education authority in connection with running an Emergency Training Scheme. The range of courses then offered by the college included a three-year programme for young people leaving school who wished to train immediately as music specialist teachers, a supplementary course for ordinary or emergency trained teachers wishing to specialise in music teaching, and a one-year course for trained musicians wanting to teach in schools and qualify for Burnham rates of pay. All this had been approved by the Ministry of Education.

In addition to the full-time courses of training colleges, there was a plethora of vacation courses. For example, at Stockwell Training College, the school music training course held by the Music Teachers' Association 'had the charm and grace of a country-house party' (*Music in Education*, May-June 1948, 37-8). Amongst the offerings at the course were Watkins Shaw on 'A Practical Music Syllabus for the Junior School', Frederick Green on 'Voice, Ear and Eye Training', and Doris Gould on 'Percussion Bands'. In addition Dorothy Smith spoke about music in the infant school, Edgar Hunt on the recorder, and Leslie Russell on the London Plan on School Music.

All this activity was, no doubt, felt to be admirable. Noel Hale, however, confessed himself worried by the sheer variety of approaches that were being recommended (*Music in Education*, September-October 1948). He called for a period of stability:

> How much of all the music-making that is going on is the result of steady research and conviction, and how much the reaction of war and unrest, of people rushing with such urgency from blood and tears to something more comforting? (Ibid., 102)

In his opinion it was the word stability that was crucial, ensuring that music as part of a liberal education reached every child, for whose training, as taxpayers, we pay. Hale enumerated the necessary conditions for such stability:

the institution of the whole of music in the educational curriculum; the provision of teachers' training facilities in line with those teachers of other subjects (in other words, full-time courses, not 'vacation spasms'); equal professional status, remuneration and representation for music teachers; provision of adequate equipment; and opportunities for students to enter the music profession.

These post-Second World War years appear to have been, for music teachers at least, a time of coming to terms with new approaches and possibilities including the expansion of instrumental teaching, and the increasing influence of the popular media. The Emergency Training Colleges forced a reassessment of the practicality of the training process. Increasing the effectiveness of music teacher training was becoming a priority.

3. 1973-1974

1974 marked the election of Wilson's Labour government, first with no overall majority, and on a second election with a majority of three. The year saw the miners' victory and also the country on the brink of the economic recession caused by the oil crisis of the previous year (Simon, 1991). The Labour manifesto of 1974 was ambitious educationally: a national system of nursery schools; big expansion of facilities for 16-to-19-year-olds; the end of the eleven plus and plans to speed up comprehensivisation; and tax relief for private schools to be withdrawn. Attention needs to be drawn, because of their profound influence during these years, to two highly significant educational reports which had been been published in the 1960s: the Newsom Report of 1963, *Half Our Future*, which focused on the implications of the raising of the school leaving age (ROSLA) from 15 to 16, and the Plowden Report of 1967, *Children and their Primary Schools*, which emphasised the importance of process and experience in learning.

The priority given by Plowden to the centrality of the child's present experience is reflected in the ascendancy of creative music making in schools during the 1970s. It was fast becoming the new orthodoxy. Creativity became a keyword in justifications for music in the curriculum. Propelled by the publication of *Sound and Silence* (Paynter and Aston, 1970), the columns of the periodicals were peppered with references to it and the Schools Council project, 'Music in the Secondary School Curriculum'. In *Music Teacher* (May 1974) we find an advertisement for a course run by the University of York, 'New Music in Action', designed for teachers of music, dance and drama. The course contributors read like a roll-call of the movement: Harrison Birtwistle, Wilfrid Mellers, Bernard Rands, Trevor Wishart, George Self and John Paynter. In addition there was an advertisement (*Music Teacher*, September 1974) for a one-term course in Creative Music Making designed for non-specialist teachers in primary schools, for which the Department of Education and Science had given its stamp of approval.

If we examine opinion in the 1970s about the purposes of music in education, there was a preoccupation with the quality of the musical process for its own sake. However this was not in the utilitarian sense of the 1920s, with its association with learning the basics of musical skills, but rather with the notion of aesthetic education.

'Aesthetic' is a keyword in the 1970s, although we noted its use by MacPherson in 1924. It was an idea that permeated a series of articles by Keith Swanwick entitled 'Class Music in the Secondary School: A Perspective' which appeared in *Music Teacher* (March-June 1974). Swanwick developed his ideas as a response to the feeling of crisis that was afflicting secondary music teachers, caused by the barrage of criticism in the wake of the Schools Council *Enquiry One* (1968), itself prompted by the Newsom Report, in which music, in the opinion of young school leavers, was the most boring and useless subject on the school curriculum.

Swanwick (*Music Teacher*, March 1974) attempted to clarify the nature of musical activity by identifying its three vital processes. First, the sounds we use in music are selected from an enormous range of possibilities; second, we have to engage in the process of relating sounds together; finally, and most crucial of all, is the intention that there shall be music:

> Just as the pumpkin and the mice are transformed into a coach and four, so our raw sounds cease to be aural materials and become charged with meaning to which we respond. And our response is an aesthetic response. (Ibid.,12)

Swanwick then elucidated the meaning of 'aesthetic': the ability to perceive and feel something which becomes self-enriching, a response to something on its own terms. Although music may be a part of cultural heritage, and is a skill-learning activity, nevertheless its central core is the aesthetic experience: music without aesthetic qualities 'is like a fire without heat' (ibid., 13). Teachers of music are inevitably involved in an aesthetic activity:

> the answer to the question 'how much music was there in the last lesson?' will be a measure of a teacher's own achievement and in part an indication of the warmth of his own aesthetic fires. (Ibid.)

It would be misleading however to characterise the seventies as single-minded as far as aims and purposes were concerned. Music literacy was a central theme of William Salaman, in a series of articles in *Music Teacher* in 1974, based upon a systematic approach to the classroom orchestra. His purpose was severely practical: how to cater for a succession of classes of 30 pupils in a relentless flow. His solution was to design over 25 carefully graded pieces for recorders, glockenspiels and xylophones, harmonicas/melodicas, and guitars, in addition to orchestral instruments. These pieces thus provided an active method of acquiring musical literacy.

Undoubtedly the notion of the aesthetic and its connection with musical creativity marked a watershed in the development of music as a school subject. Something needed to be developed because there was a sense of crisis about what actually went on in music classrooms, particularly in secondary schools.

But what was going on in schools? We gather an awareness of the problems of the music classroom and the music teacher, although at a distance, through reading two series of articles by George Odam and Keith Swanwick.

George Odam commenced his pair of articles on 'Music in the Secondary School' (*Music Teacher*, January, February 1974) with a striking image. He recollected the interviews he had conducted with prospective student music teachers, which contained conversations such as

Music was boring at school until exam work started. The thing that excites me about becoming a music teacher is that I want to make it more interesting for the younger forms - not just singing and hymn practice. (*Music Teacher*, January 1974, 9)

And Odam tells us

I watch the tree behind the bright young candidate dropping its yellow leaves and looking to winter. (Ibid.)

What depressed him was that such students found their musical salvation not in the music curriculum but in private teaching and extra-curricular activities. He located the reason for this state of affairs with music teachers. For the first time when dealing with examination work his/her true musical skills come into play; the teacher no longer becomes a performer 'capturing interest for half-an-hour like candy-floss on a stick, and the same durability' (ibid.). Instead, individuals are helped to learn and are guided step by step. The emotional and physical demands in teaching music, Odam pointed out, were immense. In order to cope, music teachers clutched at the straws of tradition:

The legacy we have inherited from Guido d'Arezzo through Sarah Glover, Curwen, and all kinds of music educators, is that we are well able to deal with large numbers with little expenditure on equipment. This is achieved by the most inefficient, wearing, tedious and primitive process in education, rote learning, and that's what many of us spend our time promulgating. (Ibid., 10)

It was Odam's conviction that pupils should be taught to read music, and for this we needed decent classroom instruments, which would act as teaching machines. He believed there were agonising choices ahead which would require Herculean strength. But unless some way was found out of the labyrinth, in Tippett's words: 'this island is going to sink into the Sea - and leave no wrack behind' (Ibid.).

In his follow-up article (*Music Teacher*, February 1974) he maintained that whilst music may be the worst-taught subject on the secondary school curriculum, it did not have less skilled or talented teachers than other subjects. There were some hopeful signs on the horizon, particularly the advent of classroom orchestras which could do much to teach basic music literacy. But Odam also outlined alternative ways of doing things. Why try to teach everything at once? Why not split classes into groups or modules? He drew parallels to the current vogue for language labs, revolutionised through electronics:

> imagine a group of nine or so working with equipment through headphones, another six at a string class with the peripatetic, four practising clarinet quartets, six occupied by listening to selected and prepared cassette tapes through stereo headphones and reading and answering prepared sheets of questions or information, and the rest working on a new creative project. (Ibid., 17)

Odam then outlined current approaches which worked badly, and they give an insight into classroom practice at the time:

> They occur particularly in schools which embrace 'creative' music in such a wholehearted fashion that lessons end up with four or five groups working against each other with the frustrated teacher dashing to and fro trying to keep things together and emerging at the end looking like Tom soon after Jerry has caught him inside a large ringing bell. (Ibid.)

Paynter and Aston's *Sound and Silence* (1970) had become, according to Odam, the equivalent of the *New English Bible*, but the problem was that music teachers ended up with too much sound and not enough silence.

Odam concluded his hard-hitting pair of articles with five points:

- the traditional music lesson of singing, listening and a bit of theory was 'as moribund as Marley';
- music teachers must find a way of passing on their knowledge at first hand to individuals;
- instruments in class are essential to gain musical literacy;
- educational technology should be exploited and should help 'the teacher to free himself from the role of compere and disc jockey'; and
- creative work should increase in demand both in quality and time as children get older, and must be carefully taught.

His parting shot was addressed to music teachers:

If at a stroke everything outside the classroom was removed by the Minister in a desperate economy measure (and it might not be far off!) would you stand with pride by what goes on in music time? Does 3B really know more than 1B, and can you measure it? Should it be necessary to work every lunch-hour, break and after school to make your subject work in the curriculum? (*Music Teacher*, February 1974, 17)

Like Odam, Swanwick identified the present moment as being a crisis for music in schools. Swanwick believed that now was the time to act decisively: either stop music as a class activity, or develop a sense of purpose about it. His three scenarios of poor teaching focusing upon unguided exploration, novelty and pupil generated work, shed light on fairly common practice:

after an hour the children are still listlessly exploring, bored to tears by an activity that has neither skill achievement nor aesthetic content ... The teacher does not know the transformation spell of selection, relation and intention, and so is not able to change the drab Cinderella of sound materials into a beautiful Princess, a musical experience. (*Music Teacher*, March 1974, 13)

when in doubt change the activity ... so activities are launched on waves of enthusiasm and as they degenerate other verses are sent off down the slipway ... I have seen more classes driven to distraction by monotonous strings of novelties without any feeling of achievement or musical purpose than by whole periods spent on a single activity. (*Music Teacher*, May 1974, 20)

where we assume that classes can be split into groups and sent off into various rooms and corners to make their own music ... without first establishing a starting point. (Ibid.)

As a consequence of reading Swanwick's article a music teacher wrote a letter to the editor of *Music Teacher* (August 1974) confessing that she felt angry and ashamed. It nicely encapsulates the frenetic pace of the period, and much of the underlying frustration of music teachers:

I have allowed my judgement to be clouded by an over-riding desire to stimulate interest ... I am a slave to the Top Twenty every Sunday. During my lessons, the tape recorder lies visible on my desk - blatant bribery, a fifteen minute reward after one hour of flogging one dead horse after another. I weep to see a trunk load of broken instruments, quite beyond repair ... I twang on a wretched guitar, and seethe when a very expensive copy of modern folk songs is stolen. I never liked them - but still - why worry? ... 'Improvisation and composition' - this produces a hollow laugh. I have found all Hell let loose when fifth year boys (ROSLA's first products) found a way into the Music Room and blew and banged everything available ... 'listening skills' - who listens? There is an all-pervading restlessness; desks and chairs are constantly on the move as ungainly bodies shift uneasily. As teachers we are reduced almost entirely to dependence on personality values. Combine a forceful personality, a strong physique, boundless nervous energy, unlimited time and ingenuity, and one has a chance of survival - with some success ... The fact remains that this teacher at least, is a weak echo of what she might be, both in enthusiasm and consequently in achievement. (Ibid., 17)

It is clear that the early 1970s were years of crisis in music education. Notions of creativity and aesthetics proved to be a heady brew which promised to deliver a musical education that was geared to feelings and personal responses: alienation might be countered. Yet in practice music teachers found it difficult to manage. There was no doubt about the excitement of the ideas, yet the transition from the rhetoric to the general practice was problematic. But it would be misleading to portray this time as single-minded. There were still voices from such respected figures as Odam and Salaman calling for a more traditional approach which met the needs of pupils and teachers.

4. 1998-1999

1998 witnessed the landslide victory of 'New' Labour, headed by Tony Blair. From an educational perspective the previous Conservative government had brought about, according to Michael Barber (1996), progress in four important respects: funding was successfully delegated to schools; national standards were established; public accountability was demanded; and the producer stranglehold on policy was loosened.

Four highly powerful educational quangos were set up in the 1990s, all of which were given partial responsibility for the governance of the teaching profession: the Teacher Training Agency (1994), the School Curriculum and Assessment Authority (1993), the Office for Standards in Education (1992), and the School Teachers Review Body (1991).

The new government inherited the National Curriculum, which was a provision of the 1988 Education Reform Act. Music managed to secure a place in this curriculum as a foundation subject. The priority of the new government lay in developing the effective teaching of the 'basics' in primary schools, which were identified as literacy and numeracy. Their enhanced status in turn threatened the presence of such subjects as music. All this was part of a larger picture of cutbacks in the arts. The findings of the Royal Society of Art's *The Disappearing Arts* (1998) were noted in *Music Teacher* (January 1999): initial teacher training was paying ever less attention to the arts; only

1 per cent of the Teacher Training Agency's three-year contracts were for the arts; only 19 out of 390 specialist secondary schools were specialising in the arts. No wonder the report concluded 'the arts are in retreat'.

It was music however that caught the headlines. The front page of *The Times Educational Supplement* on 24 April 1998 reported: 'Primary music in decline.' A 'horrifying' survey had uncovered that one in five primary schools in England and Wales was cutting down on music, and some were dropping the subject altogether. There was no doubt about the culprit: it was the government's insistence that schools concentrate on the teaching of numeracy and literacy. In the same issue the editorial was entitled 'Let the Music Play'. In addition to the curriculum issues it drew attention to the problems surrounding instrumental tuition. The *TES* mounted a campaign to save music in schools entitled 'Music for the Millennium':

> to ensure that all primary children receive their entitlement to learn about, and learn to love, music ... We want to see each one given the chance to learn an instrument ... otherwise there is a danger that too many in the next generation will be excluded from music making. (Ibid.)

One of the principal protagonists in the campaign was the conductor Sir Simon Rattle who called the present cuts 'the betrayal of an entire generation' (*TES*, 15 May 1998). As a member of the National Advisory Committee on Creative and Cultural Education, he warned Chris Smith, the Minister of Culture, that he was 'going to be hearing a lot from me, and he might find some of it uncomfortable'. Rattle spoke of his personal indebtedness to the musical benefits of the state system. One of his fears was that music in British schools could go the same way as in America where the subject was 'totally unimportant and marginalised'. Rattle concluded with an evocation of a supposedly golden age:

> School music education has been one of our glories, and for forty years our youth orchestras have been the lifeblood of music making and the envy of the world. Over the past five years we have seen all these achievements damaged.

A month after the *TES* campaign commenced, the Secretary of State for Education and Employment, David Blunkett, addressed the issue (*TES*, 22 May 1998). He expressed his own belief in the power of music, and in the necessity for each school to possess the resources to teach music. Moreover, every child should be provided with the opportunity to learn a musical instrument. Blunkett guaranteed that music would remain a compulsory subject in the National Curriculum. He proposed that ringfenced money for local musical services would be provided through a Standards Fund, and this would be topped up by the Department for Education and Employment. Consequently music would be moved from a position of decline in the 1980s to a position where it would flourish. All sorts of new initiatives were listed: 40 more specialist schools; out-of-school study centres which would offer musical opportunities; a task force on creative and cultural education. Schools needed to ensure that more time was afforded to music, so that it became a central subject on the curriculum. Blunkett admitted that his priorities lay with the raising of standards in the 3 Rs, but music could help in this, and as part of a cross-curricular approach, contribute to numeracy teaching.

Reaction to this was mostly positive, with Larry Westland from Music Industries declaring 'This is just the signal we have been waiting for. Top-slicing to protect central music services is something we have wanted for many years' (*TES*, 22 May 1998). The decline in funding was itemised: spending on music services by local education authorities had declined from £100m in 1990 to £30m today. However, Richard Hickman from the Federation of Music Services wondered whether the new proposals would really deliver equality of access. He pointed to the fate of the Norfolk Instrumental Scheme, about which a correspondent from the Service wrote 'Our slogan in recent years has been "Hang on until Labour gets in, then things will be better"- we cannot believe what is happening now' (*TES*, 19 June 1998).

Disappointing prospects for instrumental teaching were reported in a survey of LEA provision (*TES*, 24 July 1998). One in three authorities did not believe the new funding arrangements would make a difference in the uptake of vocal or instrumental tuition. Sunderland spoke of its policies in this respect as 'the application of elastoplasts'. An outlay of up to £2m was needed to revitalise just one provider. The survey went on to highlight the fact that more than half of the LEAs delegated funding for instrumental teaching to schools, moreover fewer than one in ten pupils received weekly instrumental tuition in England. This compared badly with the numbers of pupils receiving instrumental lessons in Wales and Scotland. The implications for instrumental teachers in England were that fewer full timers were being employed.

All this was evident in the effect of declining resources on British youth orchestras, often seen as the great achievement of British music education. Keith Horsfall, conductor of the Dudley Schools Symphony Orchestra saw youth orchestras

> at the apex, the top of the league ... But if we ignore music in schools, we're building on sand: everything will collapse. (*TES*, 18 December 1998)

Good news however came from the government in its detailed announcement concerning funding of instrumental music (*TES*, 29 January 1999). Hard-pressed LEAs were to get an extra £180m, doubling their funding. Existing services were to be protected with £30m and new provision of £60m would be applied to expansion and the establishment of new centres. In addition the

Youth Music Trust would extend access in and out of school, and would advise the Department for Education and Employment on quality. All this reflected a collaboration between government ministers, David Blunkett and Chris Smith.

But in the meantime the concerns about 'the disappearing arts' in primary schools, touched upon at the beginning of this section, surfaced in respect of teacher training (*TES*, 20 November 1998). Art, music and drama courses were disappearing fast; the number of trainees in music was down 23 per cent on the previous year's decline of 16 per cent. This appeared symptomatic of a 'vicious downward spiral'. All was not well with secondary recruitment either, with music underachieving by 16 per cent, and in 1998-1999 probably by 23 per cent.

Thus we see that the crisis of music education in the UK was principally focused on the decline of the instrumental teaching service, in the provision of music in primary schools, and in the supply of teacher recruits.

In spite of the perceived threat to music in schools, the *TES* (22 May 1998) reported that David Blunkett had a considerable personal commitment to music. It had played an important part in his own life and he wanted young people to have access to its enormous benefits:

> Learning an instrument, singing, or simply enjoying the music of others, can help develop an awareness of the spiritual dimension of life.

He believed it was important to draw upon the 'tremendous history' of folk music and ballad writing, so that the understanding of our culture might be reinforced.

What generally characterised the search for a convincing justification for music during this time was an exploration of the transfer of learning. In the first issue of the *TES* campaign to save music in schools, Anthony Everitt wrote an extended article entitled 'Cerebral Software' (24 April 1998) in which he drew upon recent research which explored the fundamentals of music. What distinguished music from the other arts was that it was more than art: 'It reaches beyond aesthetics into ethics and the nature of intelligence.' Everitt tells us there is nothing new in this: Plato had elaborated on the profound impact music exerted upon our individual personalities. But what was new, according to Everitt, was that scientific research demonstrated that music played a key role in the functioning of the brain. Behavioural psychologists had demonstrated how music could aid the learning process. Consequently Everitt concluded that giving more time to the 3 Rs was counter-productive if it led to fewer music classes. In other words music is fundamental to human experience:

> Underneath the elaborations of civilised life and the birth of reason lies music - the primary language. It is only as we grow up that it dwindles into an art. We forget at our peril its original underpinning function as cerebral software. (Ibid.)

In similar vein Diana Spencer (*TES*, 1 May 1998) asked: is there any impartial evidence that music lessons boost performance in other subjects? She drew on *The 4th 'R'* (MEC, 1998) a publication from the Campaign for Music in the Curriculum, which found that learning music from an early age helped children improve in a number of areas: performance in reading, maths, science and engineering; fluency in speaking their own and foreign languages; team work and social skills; memorising; reasoning; management of time; problem solving; ability to cope with stress; and artistic ability. There were specific examples quoted: primary pupils at Rhode Island, USA, made better progress in reading and maths as a result of an enhanced arts curriculum including the teaching of music; at the University of California researchers concluded that music modifies the circuits in the brain, leading to improved thinking skills.

A critical view of this notion of transferability was raised in a letter from Richard Staines which accused Everitt of simplistic assumptions and errors (*TES*, 15 May 1998). Everitt's approval of some Swiss research into the benefits of extended music teaching was challenged, because in fact the supposed benefits were of an affective nature rather than in effects which were tangible, measurable and scholastic. This particular debate continues.

The two most apparent curriculum innovations within music chronicled in *Music Teacher* have been music technology and popular music. Adrian York in his article 'Be Brave about the new sound world' (*Music Teacher*, February 1999) encouraged music teachers to put in the time and effort needed to embrace technology. After all, many children have access to electronic keyboards or PCs with relatively sophisticated sequencing, sampling and editing software. The technophobia felt by many music educators may be unsurprising but it has to be addressed for three reasons: undoubted demand from pupils; to break the out-moded chain of music education; and to accept the primacy of popular musical culture, itself permeated by technology, in the twenty-first century. York's conclusion was hard-hitting:

> The present education establishment is too locked into the past to understand the future and will end up being marginalised, and yet, despite this lack of leadership it can be an exciting and creative time for music teachers if we grasp the opportunities the new technologies offer to help deliver highly trained and motivated young musicians. (Ibid., 22)

Popular culture was also emphasised in an article by Norton York (*Music Teacher*, April 1999), who pointed to New Labour as a party which seemed to understand the economic importance of popular music. But music educators should feel confident with the progress they had made in opening up the music room and curriculum to pop, particularly through GCSE. York was a founder member of Rock School in the early nineties, set up to provide some clear standards for playing pop which teachers and pupils could use as an accurate measure of achievement. York calls for a debate about music teacher-training and how it may need to adapt to the musical aesthetic of pop, as well as to its technology.

But *Music Teacher* also witnessed a good deal of support for traditional music teaching. In particular Andrew Peggie, a respected music educator, wrote an impassioned letter (January 1999) protesting about the obsession the National Curriculum had with an inclusive, maximum breadth approach, which resulted in virtually no progression and even less context. He suggested three strategies: to ensure all pupils develop a confident vocal identity through speech, singing and movement; to ensure pupils experience a wide range of music through listening, implying that curriculum music reverts to music-appreciation; and to ensure pupils achieve Grade 5 level fluency in reading notation by the end of key stage 3. He was not alone in raising the vexed question of notation teaching.

As part of its 'Music for the Millennium' campaign the *TES* focused on schools which provided exemplars of good practice, frequently drawing on schools identified as outstanding by OFSTED Inspectors. These examples illustrate a more positive view of inclusiveness fostered by the National Curriculum than Peggie's more negative stance. For example, Kates Hill School in Dudley had a music programme that influenced other crucial areas of the curriculum. Its Head stated:

> We were worried about six year olds' standard of writing, and as a special project we did the whole of the year's writing work through music, using good song books with children writing linking narrative between the songs and stories. We were aiming for level 2s that year, and in fact we got more level 3s than ever before. People should not think you can only deliver the literacy hour through literacy type work. (*TES*, 1 May 1998)

The school encouraged Year 6 pupils to write compositions from scratch, using percussion, electronic keyboards, ethnic instruments and music software. A multi-cultural approach was fostered through the Asian Dance Group, and the school steel band which, it was claimed, had saved some pupils from exclusion.

A secondary school that was singled out was the Duchesses' County High School in Alnwick, Northumberland (*TES*, 22 May 1999). With a choir of 90 pupils including 40 boys, there is an apparent sense of commitment, and a repertoire ranging from Zulu songs to the songs of Andrew Lloyd-Webber, and from Tammy Wynette to Vivaldi. GCSE numbers have increased from 20 to 70 in three years. The secret appears to be the music teacher's sheer commitment and conviction:

If you believe, as I do, that music is the most important subject you can teach, then you do everything you can to give it rigour in the classroom. I work out the structure of lessons and plan progression extremely carefully. I expect pupils to be with me 100 per cent. (Ibid.)

But as far as the plight of music teachers was concerned there was the serious worry that too few music graduates were becoming classroom music teachers. Tony Knight of the Qualifications and Curriculum Authority (QCA) (*Music Teacher*, April 1999) outlined five factors that might dissuade a youngster from entering the music teaching profession: the hugely exhausting balance of curricular and extra-curricular work; the isolation of frequently being a one-person department; the low status of the subject in schools; ineffective timetabling for the subject; and poor resources and accommodation. His conclusion was that the nature of the job and attitudes towards it needed to change before more young people were attracted to it.

In these years music was again in crisis, with threats to its status as a curriculum subject. Fortunately by the end of 1999 the *TES* was welcoming music's return to the primary school National Curriculum (26 November 1999). There was a greater emphasis upon justifying the subject through 'transferability', but undoubtedly it has been IT and the connected popular music revolution that have spurred on music to its latest developments. If the school inspectors are to be believed, the National Curriculum has given rise to much encouraging practice. The contrary view, however, is that it has played its part in 'dumbing down' the subject.

5. Conclusion

What arises from this survey is that the 75 years or so under consideration have witnessed struggles between groups representing different conceptions of what musical experiences should be embodied in the curriculum, and to what ends the curriculum in music should be directed. These historical snapshots have served as an introduction to the period and its battles. But they are not enough. The next four chapters provide the detail which underlies the process of curriculum reform, and the ways in which new ideas are implemented or resisted by both teachers and policy makers.

3 'Changing the Face of School Music': Walford Davies and the Development of BBC School Music Broadcasts 1924-1947

On 12 January 1930, Walford Davies (1869-1941) wrote a letter to *The Times* expressing the conviction that only when an efficient wireless and gramophone room had become a matter of routine equipment in every school would we be able to establish music firmly throughout national life. Although this was a long-term prospect, he declared there were a thousand musical pioneers using the new media, 'already changing the face of school music' (BBC Written Archives, 1929-1936, 11 February, 1930).

A few years before this letter was published, the *School Music Review* (September 1925) drew attention to ways in which the new technologies might help alleviate the chronic shortage of music teachers. In particular it made reference to H.G. Wells's book *The Salvaging of Civilisation* (1921), which looked forward to 'the machining of education' (ibid., 156). Such a development might take the drudgery out of teaching and herald the dawn of 'the schooling of the world'. The *School Music Review* suggested that some few inspired and inspiring teacher-musicians might design prepared lessons with suitable music examples and exercises utilising the new apparatus. Through such an economical and efficient process, the average teacher would be provided with 'a comparatively impeccable means of conveying knowledge to all children' (ibid., 106). All this might help to deal with the music teacher shortage.

New technologies were becoming widely available for music educators in Great Britain in the years after the First World War. In 1919 the Education Department of the Gramophone Company was established (Scholes, 1947, 790), and the transmission of the first school broadcast, whose subject happened to be music by the British Broadcasting Company (BBC), was in April 1924. The new educational possibilities were seized enthusiastically by Davies: the radio and gramophone were 'Walford's two great instruments in alliance' (Allsobrook, 1992, 94).

This chapter is primarily concerned with the development of school music broadcasts which between the 1920s and early 1940s were dominated by Walford Davies. I shall first present a brief biography of Davies, and an outline of his educational thinking, followed by an account of his work with the Gramophone Company, in which he initiated ideas that were to shape his broadcasts. The central section of the chapter comprises a detailed study of Davies's school music broadcasts and their reception by the music programme sub-committee of the Central Council for School Broadcasting. In order to provide a contrasting account of alternative strategies in school music broadcasts I focus on the work of two broadcasters who developed distinctive programmes: Ann Driver and *Music and Movement*, and Herbert Wiseman and *Singing Together.* I shall consider critical reactions to school music broadcasts and shall offer some conclusions about the effectiveness of broadcasting in changing the face of school music. Finally I shall evaluate the significance of Davies's contribution to the wider context of the national musical life.

1. Walford Davies

Born in Oswestry in 1869, Davies received his musical education as a chorister at St George's Chapel, Windsor, and later was a student of Parry and Stanford at the Royal College of Music. He started to build a considerable reputation as a choir trainer at the Temple Church, London, and as a composer. In 1918 he was organiser of musical activity for the Royal Air Force in France, and the following year was appointed Professor of Music at Aberystwyth and Director of the Welsh National Council for Music (Allsobrook, 1992). After a hectic number of years spent revitalising Welsh music he returned as organist to St George's Chapel in 1926, and in 1934 succeeded Elgar as the Master of the King's Musick (Colles, 1942).

Davies was a larger-than-life character. The title of his book, *The Pursuit of Music* (1935), conveys his restless nature and hurly-burly existence (Allsobrook, 1992, 69). Reactions to him were extreme: to some he was a cultural hero, to others he was sanctimonious and narrow. There seemed little room for compromise.

Musically he was conservative. According to Stradling and Hughes (1993) he was part of a group, clustered around Parry, intent on spreading patriotism and religious feeling through music in order to counter modern influences which were seen to result in musical anarchy and destruction. Not only did Davies not like contemporary music, he was allergic to Grand Opera! (Robertson, 1961, 208). It is significant that he conducted the first performance of Parry's patriotic hymn, *Jerusalem*, in 1916 at a 'Fight for Right' congress, an organisation from which Parry later withdrew because of its half-truths and jingoism (Banfield, 1985, and Debble, 1992). This conservatism was also apparent in his work with the BBC: he was the most influential member of the BBC Music Advisory Committee, which acted as a severe brake on the BBC Music Department's progressive policies which favoured contemporary music (Kenyon, 1981).

We have to reconcile Davies's musical conservatism with his burning desire to communicate with ordinary people, and his willingness to campaign for access to musical experience. His early song collections demonstrate something of this, including several for serving soldiers fighting at the Front (Davies, 1915a, b, 1916). Most popular of all these collections was his *Fellowship Song Book* (1915c). The sponsoring organisations for this volume demonstrate some of his populist sympathies: The National Adult School Union, The Co-operative Holidays Association, The Holiday Fellowship, The Workers Educational Association, The Home Study Union. He wanted such a song book to be used at 'public meetings, co-operative holidays, tramps on moor and shore, study circles, lecture-schools, 'firesides' and social gatherings generally' (ibid.). The anthology was hugely successful: it sold 350,000 copies and spawned *The New Fellowship Song Book* (Davies, 1931). Right up until his death Davies was centrally involved in the preparation of another widely popular musical collection, *The BBC Hymn Book* (see Wolfe, 1984: 389).

The notion of fellowship was central to his work and will be an important thread throughout my consideration of his achievement. He believed music to be an ideal school subject because it ensured the finest team work which resulted in team action (Davies, 1933a). However, his sense of fellowship had sometimes a military character.

He encouraged teachers to adopt a military organisation with the music class (Davies, 1933b). The ideal number of pupils, he reckoned, was sixteen, and there should be a system of sub-division and sub-command, with something like two NCOs (non-commissioned Officers) and platoons numbering eight children. Teams might be placed under different commanders and encouraged to sing in competition, but with 'the right spirit of friendly contest'.

What were his convictions about music education? He set down his ideas in *First Steps in Music* (1933a). His central concern was that 'rhythmic melody' could be regarded as a veritable mother tongue. He pointed to children who could rap out a rhythm and develop four-phrase tunes: he had received such examples from four-year olds.

At the heart of his thinking, however, was the belief that written sounds were a trifle compared with the experience of the thing itself. The priority was first to teach children by ear, encouraging hearty team singing, then cultivating a decent tone, and developing the ability to sing at sight. But he was adamant that only when musical construction and design were addressed would 'the full Hamlet' be achieved. Therefore children should be given the chance to design their own small tunes. They should be expected to write them, just as they were expected to write essays.

But Davies realised the frequently daunting difficulties in schools. There was a vicious circle: 19-year-old students in training colleges were merely like nine-year-olds when they came to music. Gramophone recordings and radio broadcasts held the promise that they would be able to help overcome the seemingly intractable problem of providing a basic and effective music curriculum for all children in school capable of being taught by classroom teachers.

2. The Gramophone Company and Walford Davies

In his entertaining autobiography, *More than Music* (1961), Alec Robertson tells how, after the First World War, he was earning his living as a music appreciation lecturer for the London County Council when he heard that the Gramophone Company (His Master's Voice) was proposing to start a new department to propagate the use of the gramophone in schools, and, having appointed a head of department, they wanted a musician to go about the country as 'a sort of superior salesman' (ibid., 112). He got the job and in general met a great many musicians who were snobbish about the new development, but there were a few that appreciated the possibilities, including Walford Davies.

Davies's earliest sound recordings specifically made for schools were a series of *Melody Lectures* recorded in 1922 (Davies, 1922): this was before the days of electrical recording in the mid-1920s (Chanan, 1995). The lectures were the first set of teaching records issued by HMV. There were twelve lectures in all, comprising nine double-sided records, including three containing supplementary and illustrative material. Davies played the piano and provided the commentary, with Marjorie Hayward playing the violin. They present a method of teaching that was an integral part of Davies's scheme of musical training in Welsh schools (*The Voice*, 1922, 3). The method remained constant throughout Davies's recording and broadcasting career.

In the first lecture, 'On Musical Outline', Davies emphasised the importance of listening:

> You have heard the old saying 'eyes and no eyes', and if you know what that means you will understand exactly what is meant by 'ears and no ears'... Human beings look with their eyes, they seldom look with their ears ... We must learn to look with our ears at melody if we are to trace its meaning. (Ibid., Transcription (hereinafter (T)) C1063)

The next steps were to define sound, music, musician, a note, an interval, a chord, and rhythm.

The third lecture focused on the pentatonic scale: 'you will be writing literally on the scale of the world ... the heavenly scale' (ibid., (T) C1064). But melodies had to be invested with personal meaning:

> Let us call you at once into the unseen world of sound in your mind and give it a meaning as best as you can ... I believe melody is the really mother tongue of everyone. English and Welsh and all other local languages will die ages before melody can die ... It is the natural language of everybody all the world over, just because it is so straight and clear and beautiful, a way of uttering what we mean and feel. (Ibid., 7)

Thus, Davies was able to use the gramophone to preach powerfully on the implications of music as a universal language. It may not be too fanciful to connect this with a quest for an organic society, utilising the new medium.

Pupils were provided with an ABC of tune building: Adventure, Balance and Completion. Technical hints included: attempt to rise or fall by step; leap by a firm interval; return within it. Davies contrasted a line in drawing with a line in melody:

> You will always find a line in music different from a line in drawing in this very way, that is like a line of advance from point to point almost like a railway line, always like a thought. (Ibid., (T) C1065)

He reminded his students of the need for balance, completion and cadence. He was always the master of the appropriate simile:

> The cadence is really like the pillar to a suspension bridge, it keeps the melody up, but its long spans of melody are loveliest. (Ibid., (T) C1067)

Of particular interest in the series is the supplementary disc devoted to 'Tunes built in Wales', with four tunes taken from elementary school pupils, and four from adult students from Davies's summer schools (ibid., C1069). They were played by Marjorie Hayward and Walford Davies who also harmonised them and provided a running commentary. Davies's final words in this series were:

> I hope they [the lectures] will cause you to try to make up a hundred beautiful melodies of your own ... Try at least to make one a week. Write what you love to write and balance it up and complete it ... remember that trying to write oneself is the greatest possible help towards listening well to the perfect melodies that are in the world, waiting for us all to enjoy them. (Ibid., (T) C1068)

The Gramophone Company's house magazine, *The Voice* (1922), impressed upon the record dealers the originality of these recordings: nothing like them had been issued before. Consequently special window displays should be arranged in towns Davies was likely to visit; after all he was a 'celebrity artist'. However, the magazine (and presumably Davies) was a little coy about the notion of children as composers:

> We should like to clear up a misunderstanding that seems to have got abroad. Dr Davies has no intention or wish of making us all composers. He uses the composition method as a means for us to obtain a grasp of the art of music, whereby we shall be able to proceed to acquire a full understanding of all the music there is in the world. (Ibid., 4)

In 1929 a new series was released taking advantage of the new electrical recording techniques. It was modelled closely upon the old version, but more conversational and informal in tone and renamed *Twelve Talks on Melody* (Davies, 1929b). It was intended for a wider audience:

> When the time came for newly recording the originals, it was clear that twelve informal talks ... would make for more serviceable records than more formal lectures. So now they have been wholly recast for the general arm-chair listener into a conversational ... mould, though their use for teaching purposes in advanced classes has been born in mind. (Davies, 1929a, 5)

Although the sequence of talks is almost exactly the same as the 1922 lecture series, the supplementary illustrated records were different and did not include 'Tunes Built in Wales' (Davies, 1929b). In the correspondence with the Gramophone Company it is interesting to observe Davies's concern that the significance of the new series would be underplayed (Letter to Mr Lack from Walford Davies, 8 October 1929, EMI Music Archives). He was disturbed to learn that the records were to be issued as optional to dealers. This seemed to imply to him that they were merely to be regarded as 'an educational stunt'. But Davies insisted that they would make a wide appeal to the man-in-the-street; indeed they would make a thoroughly sound family Christmas present. There was a reassuring reply:

> I have intimated to the English branch that in addition to these records being compulsory, there should be a streamer which will be put out on November 1st so that it can be hung or pasted on windows on the premises of our dealers ... this streamer should include your photograph printed on, as this I am sure would be of very great value in the large and wide distribution of these records. (Letter from Mr Lack to Walford Davies, 9 October 1929, EMI Music Archives)

All this tends to confirm Davies's reputation as 'a hustler second to none' (*The Voice*, 1922, 4), but also as someone who was constantly trying to expand the breadth of music's appeal to a wider audience, and to build up an informed musical community.

There is no doubt that Davies's early series of recordings broke new ground, and established in the popular mind the idea that composing was open to all. It was probably the basis of the Hadow Report's observation that Davies had discovered 'an astonishing capacity for melody among the children of the Welsh schools' (Board of Education, 1926, 240).

3. The BBC

At this point we need to sketch an outline of the early history of school music broadcasting. A useful source is found in a regular column that started to appear in the monthly teachers' paper *The School Music Review* (hereinafter *SMR*) from March 1924 entitled 'Wireless News'. It was compiled by a member of the British Brodcasting Company, K.A. Wright, who was later to become an active figure in the organisation of music within the Corporation (see Briggs, 1965).

Optimism ran high. Wright informed his readers that as a result of the previous eighteen months, they should be accustomed to hearing music over the air. The new medium had a lofty purpose: 'broadcasting to the nation will be as the teacher to the child' (*SMR*, March 1924). More specifically Wright outlined some of the benefits for

> the teacher in the primary school who must, with a number of other subjects, take music in the ordinary routine. Teachers in thousands of village schools have never had the chance to attend concerts giving music, the like of which radio brings into their homes. (Ibid., 298)

However there were no school broadcasts as such. Opportunities to talk about and perform music for a youthful audience were provided by *Children's Hour*. Wright informed his readers that on almost every Wednesday 'Uncle' Jeff talked on some musical topic, with the Wireless Orchestra giving illustrations. Every Thursday evening 'Uncle' Humpty-Dumpty with 'Aunt' Hilda presented a musical talk to the 'kiddies' about Pip, a boy who underwent some music lessons over the air. Musical form, pianoforte music, rhythm and tempo were some of the topics covered. The presenters were notable figures: 'Uncle' Jeff was L. Stanton Jefferies, the Musical Director of the BBC; 'Aunt' Hilda was the distinguished pianist Hilda Dederich; 'Uncle' Humpty Dumpty was no less a figure than Wright himself (see Briggs, 1965).

Wright provides us with some detail of the content of Jefferies' talks:

He has devised a novel and effective method of initiating the young, and invisible hearers into the mysteries of Staff Notation by describing vividly ... the quaint shapes that transform themselves magically from 'an egg to a stick', to a minim then a crotchet and successfully into perky and still more perky quavers and semiquavers ... 'Uncle' Jeff's gift for turning a clef into magic telegraph wires with jolly fat birds hopping tunes on them could well be cultivated by every music teacher. (*SMR*, March 1924, 324)

These *ad hoc* arrangements were soon to be transformed with the arrival of Walford Davies into the world of the BBC.

3.1 Davies and his School Music Broadcasts

As a consequence of his work in Wales and with the Gramophone Company (Allsobrook, 1992, Chap. 7) Davies was invited to attend a meeting of the Advisory Committee on Music at the BBC in February 1924. The eloquence with which he spoke impressed the managing-director, John Reith, with the result that Davies found himself giving the first school broadcast in April (Colles, 1942, 131).

From the start there was no doubt that Davies was an inspired radio communicator. Someone who listened to one of his early broadcasts was Mary Somerville, who was to become the most powerful personality within schools broadcasting (Briggs, 1965, and Cain and Wright, 1994). She wrote memorably about the effect of that experience:

The first time that I ever heard a broadcast was by accident in a country school house where the sailor brother of the school mistress had installed a wireless set. There in her little parlour she and I and the three most musical of her pupils listened turn and turn about - for there were only two pairs of earphones - to a talk on music by Sir Walford Davies ... Things happened in all of us, in the children, in their music-loving teacher and in me. The children's eyes were round with wonder. We grown-ups were exalted. Beauty could now enter every home and every classroom. After the broadcast we made our own music, the children and their teacher played us some of the themes we had heard on the air, and then, far into the night, she and I talked of what the brave new medium of communication might mean for the schools. (Somerville, 1947, 9)

By September 1924 Davies was broadcasting to schools every Monday.

The turning point in the early years for school broadcasts came in 1927 with the publication of the Kent Report, *Educational Broadcasting* (County of Kent, 1927). This was produced as the result of a suggestion by John Reith that the Carnegie Trust might help fund an investigation into school broadcasting. The Trust agreed to do this in 1926, providing £300 for the enquiry and £1000 for wireless sets for selected elementary schools in the county of Kent.

It fell to Mary Somerville to go around the schools, seeing at first hand what was actually happening. She was to recall later that this was 'a year of eating humblepie ... We had come very near to failure, but we had at least begun to work as pioneers in radio education' (Somerville, 1947, 12). The problem was that some broadcasters did not have a knowledge of children in their bones. They did not visit schools, and they tended to talk down to the children: even Sir Walford could talk too fast and use unfamiliar metaphors.

The report contains a description of the music broadcasts planned by Davies as a two-year course between September 1926 and July 1928. Each lesson was divided into four parts: revision by playing melodies composed by the pupils as a result of previous lessons; introducing new material involving exploration of a new principle illustrated by the echo game; the singing of selected passages; a miniature concert. In the evaluation, the report found that co-operation by the teachers was not as thorough as the lecturers had the right to expect, although it noted that the teachers with no musical knowledge could operate effectively. There was a general welcome on behalf of teachers for the delivery of the lecturer, but they were not altogether satisfied that the matter of each session was grasped fully by the class. Although there was an improvement in sight singing by the third term, there was not an increase in the number of compositions or in the overall standard of community singing. Additional interest was, however, generated. It was concluded that providing a music broadcast for half-an-hour every week need not encroach upon other subjects. However, the teaching of singing and hymns should remain the responsibility of the school.

One of the far-reaching results of the report was the setting up of a permanent machinery to enable contact to take place between the BBC, the Board of Education, the Local Education Authorities, and teachers. The new body was the Central Council for School Broadcasting (CCSB), and in 1929 a network of programme sub-committees was set up which were involved in programme planning and advised the Council (Somerville, 1947). On each sub-committee

> Teachers from listening schools formed a majority in order to protect the child as indeed proved to be necessary sometimes, from the enthusiasm of their colleagues who were specialists in the subject rather than specialists in the teaching of it. (Ibid., 16)

The membership of the first music programme sub-committee comprised two members of the CCSB (including Davies), two specialist advisers (including Dr John Borland and Dr Geoffrey Shaw (HMI)), six teachers, and two members of the BBC. The minutes of this sub-committee provide us with a lot of evidence about policy making and the evaluation process (BBC Written Archives, 1929-1936, 1936-1946).

Davies's weekly transmissions were called *Elementary Music* at first, and subsequently from 1929 until 1934, *Junior* and *Senior Music Lessons.* These lessons were designed for pupils between 8-11 years and 11-14 years respectively. The nature of the broadcasts changed little over these years and kept broadly to the pattern described in the Kent Report. I shall concentrate upon this series because it best exemplifies Davies's approach to music teaching. The reader needs to bear in mind, however, that Davies was also involved in broadcasting concerts to schools.

Perhaps the two most significant parts of the broadcasts were the echo game and tune making. We have been left a tantalising recording of an eight-minute *Junior Music Lesson* which provides a vivid illustration of the echo game (BBC, n.d.). The intention of the game was to develop the ear, to relate the patterns of musical notation, and to encourage attentive listening. Davies sang a phrase and was echoed by his colleague George Dixon (who had responsibility within the BBC for the programmes). The children in the listening schools would join in with Dixon. The following extract provides a flavour and is based upon the phrases of a song which was to be sung later in the lesson, 'Dance to your daddy':

> I'll do number one three times, and you'll answer me exactly ... The second one was very soft - did you get it very soft? ... You children, the great thing is to look at the notes as you sing them with your eyes, and listen with all your ears to me, and jump into the train to get going. (Ibid., (T))

Davies placed considerable emphasis upon a musical singing style. He asked Dixon to model a phrase 'lazily' ('Oh! I've heard such a lot of singing like that!'), and then a phrase 'very, very exact and quick and lively and clear'. In listening to the broadcast what comes over is Davies's intimacy and directness:

> That's got three bars in it, I'm sorry, I must have made a mistake, I'm sorry ... What a pity it's all finished now, and we were just getting warmed to it. Never mind, I hope you enjoyed it. Good-bye. (Ibid., (T))

As in his gramophone series Davies regarded 'tune building' by children as an integral part of his work. In 1926 he had written the first BBC manual intended for children, *Melody Book No. 1* (Davies, 1926), which included space for the scholars (as they were then known) to write their own musical phrases, as well as sixteen tunes made up by children and mostly set to nursery rhyme texts. In subsequent pamphlets a regular feature of each printed lesson note was the inclusion of a tune set to words and submitted in the name of individual schools. For example, the pamphlet for 1934 (BBC, 1934) contained contributions from seven schools (although sometimes the tunes were conflated from different versions). These songs would then be taught over the air. As an aside, we see Davies's practical concern for crossing social barriers in the decision to allow old copies of the school music broadcast pamphlets to be supplied free of charge for the use of men in the unemployment clubs in Wales (June 30 1933, Music Programme Sub-Committee Minutes, BBC Written Archives, 1929-1936).

Colles (1942) outlined Davies's way of working with tune building. A phrase pattern was proposed and the children were asked to provide an answering phrase. Then they would be asked to produce a melody to a set of words. They sent in their written efforts each week, but the numbers grew to such menacing proportions that a limit had to be placed on no more than three melodies a week from each school. A dozen of the best would be played at the next lesson.

Soon after it had been instituted, the music programme sub-committee received reports from teachers that Sir Walford was often proceeding at too fast a rate. It was decided to take regular soundings of opinions through the distribution of a questionnaire to thirty teachers (11 February 1930, Music Programme Sub-Committee, BBC Written Archives, 1929-1936). The completed questionnaires revealed some strengths and weaknesses (ibid., 16 July 1930). The Echo Game was almost unanimously found to help children in the matter of sight reading, although it was suggested that some of the phrases might be made longer and more difficult and echo some well-known musical themes. Later reports focused upon tune building: 'younger listeners should be encouraged to improvise tunes while the teacher wrote them down' (ibid., 17 June 1932); scholars' tunes should not overload the lessons, perhaps only one should be played; Davies might like to deliver two holiday programmes for children on 'Children's Tunes' (ibid., 3 February 1933); some scholars had no aptitude for tune writing (ibid., 24 October 1934).

Perhaps the most perceptive critique of Davies's school broadcasts came in 1932 from his powerful colleague on the music programme sub-committee, Geoffrey Shaw (HMI):

> I do not believe we have yet arrived at the perfect form of teaching music by wireless: That it will come is more than probable. It is significant that the most attractive, perhaps of all broadcasting lecturers and speakers does not always hold the attention of pupils in particular schools. I have watched a class *endure* passively a wireless lesson from the distinguished lecturer; if the lecturer had been before them in person, that same class would have been stirred into mental activity and would have been thrilled by the personality of the lecturer ... Perhaps a wireless syllabus on a broader basis would do something to improve matters. The present one seems to some of us a little narrow and limited in scope. (Shaw, 1932)

In 1934, the year in which he succeeded Elgar as Master of the Kings Musick, Davies retired from regular school broadcasting. He was succeeded by Ernest Read and Thomas Armstrong who declared their intention of continuing Davies's pioneering work (BBC, 1934-1935). Both men followed Davies's example, and rarely deviated from their mentor's model. It was a period of stagnation.

Meanwhile, Davies remained active within broadcasting with such programmes as *Chords that Matter* and in his significant work with the Religious Broadcasting Department (Wolfe, 1984, 89) where he devised a most successful series, *Melodies of Christendom*, which lasted until 1939. It was a programme designed to improve the music in churches by aiding, on a limited technical basis, the work of choirmasters and organists: again, an example of Davies widening the scope of radio's educational impact.

On the outbreak of war in 1939 he was brought back to present the programme *Music Makers*, which continued in the tradition he had established. But critical reaction now became severe. His style was regarded as persuasive but the content was thin. The BBC Education Officer from Leeds, Joseph Smith, noted that, whilst the music teacher in the school he visited enjoyed the programme, the children were completely bored:

> I am convinced that no child could have learnt how to write music on the strength of the two or three minutes in the talk ... At the end of the broadcast I felt absolutely breathless with the variety of ideas that had been thrown at me. (29 February 1940, Memorandum from Education Officer, Leeds, Sir Walford Davies File 5b, BBC Written Archives)

Worse was to come. On 13 March 1940 the CCSB convened a special meeting to consider music broadcasts to schools. Seven music advisers, as well as representatives from the Board of Education and HMI were invited. Amongst the reported recommendations was that tune writing should be abandoned; the time could be used in better ways as most children listening could not read music satisfactorily and consequently would not be able to write it. This was a fairly constant concern in the debate about tune writing over the years. The situation was exacerbated by the absence of pamphlets, due to war-time economy. The executive committee endorsed the conference report to the effect that

> Sir Walford Davies should be asked to continue but without spending time on the writing and playing of tunes by children. (Letter from Mary Somerville to Walford Davies, 15 April 1940, Sir Walford Davies File 5b, BBC Written Archives)

An internal BBC memo stated baldly 'Sir Walford Davies to be dropped for tune writing broadcasts' (26 April 1940, Sir Walford Davies File 5b, BBC Written Archives).

Mary Somerville, Davies's erstwhile supporter, confessed that she wondered if she could rely on the opinion of the music advisers (ibid., 15 May 1940). John Horton, however, who had had responsibility for the school music broadcasts since 1937, denied that questions of personality had affected the recommendation; the committee had wanted a 'bread and butter' teaching course, and Walford Davies did not provide this (ibid., 21 May 1940). In fact, Davies did successfully try a new tack, involving teaching children to sing. He would work with a group of children one hour before the broadcast, and then present the programme based on their music making (Colles, 1942, 167). He died in 1941. For some time his experiments with children composing melodies lay apparently dormant. In John Horton's account of school music broadcasts in 1947, no mention is made of tune building (Horton, 1947).

3.2 *Ann Driver and* Music and Movement

After the resignation of Walford Davies in 1934, and possibly reacting to critical comment, the music programme sub-committee had to think of new formats. The Programme and Pamphlet Committee suggested there should be a new course for children under the age of six (28 February, 1934, Music Programme Sub-Committee, 1929-1936, BBC Written Archives). This followed a visit by Mary Somerville, the head of school broadcasts, and George Dixon, to Ann Driver who was a disciple of Jaques-Dalcroze, and who ran her own Music and Movement school (19 February 1934, Ann Driver File 1a, BBC Written Archives). As a result of the visit she pioneered the Music and Movement broadcasts.

In her book *Music and Movement* (1936) Driver put forward her ideals and her practice:

> If this development of body can be harnessed to the study of such an art as music, exercising the power of the mind to work with ease ... grace and beauty, then a unity is established which satisfies the needs of both body and soul. (Ibid., 5)

She argued that if singing was the sole medium of instruction, music education became one-sided and inadequate. Having felt rhythm in themselves children must then learn to adapt it to that of the music: 'it is the music that must evoke their movement and arouse the aesthetic sense - movement the servant of music' (ibid., 27). Musical concepts, analysis and appreciation were accumulated through bodily movement and dance. Basic rhythms, such as marching, walking, jumping, running and skipping, were taught through often improvised music. Musical phrasing and structure were expressed in dance and visual terms.

The programmes aimed at five- to seven-year-olds were immediately successful: the under-sixes in particular loved them, and many infant schools equipped themselves with a receiving set specifically for their reception (11 January 1935, Music Programme Sub-Committee, BBC Written Archives, 1929-1936). In listening to a recording of a transmission one is immediately struck by Driver's child-centred approach, and by the imaginative quality of the programme (*Music and Movement* broadcast, 6 November 1944, BBC Sound Archive). First she concentrates on outlining contrasts between heavy and light steps, and their musical equivalents. The children are asked to make big, heavy steps to the sound of the big drum, and later tip-toe steps 'light as a feather' to the little drum. To the sound of evocative improvisations on the piano the children are requested to pick up an imaginary pin from the floor and place it in a box, then to haul a heavy sack of coal onto the cart. The next step is for the children to become cart-horses pulling the cart along, and then ponies trotting. In all these ways Driver attempted to evoke responses based on feeling.

Music and Movement enthusiasts believed it essential to teach movement in association with good music, so that children received a pleasurable awareness of musical facts in association with movement. The stress on the quality of the music making was crucial. Ann Driver was able to attract the best musicians to work with her, including the Griller Quartet, because of the quality of her own musicianship (BBC, 1949). In its discussion concerning a questionnaire that had been sent out to schools the sub-committee noted that there was 'an overwhelming volume of commendation', paying particular attention to Ann Driver's 'perfect voice and delivery'. The programme promoted a 'happy and joyful atmosphere', and became 'real foundation work for maypole and folk dancing taken later'. The physical benefits were apparent: 'the children walk quite freely with no stiffness' (24 January 1936, Music Programme Sub-Committee, BBC Written Archives, 1929-1936). There were musical benefits too. Children produced a quickened response to the rhythm and character of the music.

The programme appeared to give rural schools a revelation about the possibility of linking music and movement. The music programme sub-committee agreed that a second-level *Music and Movement* course should be organised for eight- to nine-year-olds, which would include elementary teaching of pitch, sight singing and coverage of the instruments of the orchestra (ibid.). The distinction between the two levels of courses was outlined in the *BBC Annual* (1937):

> Ann Driver has adapted the technique she uses for children of five ... She makes the younger children simply beat time to the tunes they hear, but she makes the older ones pretend they have drums. The younger children imitate with the arms and hands the signs for crotchets and quavers, but the older children learn to recognise the signs when they are written on the board, and to beat out first a time and then a tune on imaginary drums, perhaps singing as well. The problem of

course is to negotiate the transition between the informal infants' work ... and the more formal instruction which comes later. (Ibid., 44)

By the following year the committee noted 'Ann Driver's excellence is taken for granted'. Children empathised with her to the extent that teachers asked that she should not say 'good-bye' at the end of programmes 'as the children feel that she is going away for good and are dejected'. The second-level course for juniors was a great success as 'clumsy boys are specially enjoying this course' (12 January 1937, Music File 1, 1936-1946, BBC Written Archives). Later, however, it was observed that Ann Driver appeared to talk down to the older children, and that there was some passivity, with pupils sitting around the blackboard (ibid., 22 March 1937). During the early days of the war the programme was increased in output to meet the needs of schools working in shifts (ibid., 13 March 1940).

What criticism there was focused upon whether a physical or a musical response was the priority. It was important to be clear about this, as apparently the programme was often confused by teachers with Physical Training (PT). (We need to recollect that Cecil Sharp's work on folk-dance in schools in the 1920s had taken place under the aegis of the Syllabus of Physical Training (see Bloomfield, 2001)). The issue was discussed by two conferences in 1944 held by the Central Council for School Broadcasting on the musical training of the young child (24 October and 1 December 1944, Music File 1, 1936-1946, BBC Written Archives). It was agreed that most people experienced a physical response whilst listening to music, and that this active expression was of great value. But, it was argued, in music teaching, attention had to be placed on the music, which used the children's natural and trained sense of movement as a means of teaching the elements of music. This is what distinguished it from PT. Whilst natural movement should be the basis of the work, a vocabulary of movement needed to be worked out. But PT teachers had been critical that the movement content was paltry and it had been left to them to correct the ensuing faults. Music teachers therefore needed to look at the quality of movement, and be careful that it was not too advanced or harmful.

Other concerns had been voiced some years earlier by a teacher from Exeter, Marion Anderson, in correspondence with *Music in Schools*. Children should be expected to relate to more definite musical facts. Knowledge of more rhythm names could lead to a greater correlation with rhythmic and percussion band work. She suggested that traditional tunes could be sung with percussion background for movement; indeed the children could dance to a percussion band (*Music in Schools*, January-February 1941).

It was Driver's achievement to develop the ideas of Jaques-Dalcroze through her broadcasts. Like Dalcroze, her emphasis was upon music. But things were to change. Gradually the ideas of Laban concerning movement and dance became more influential. These changed the emphasis. It is significant that the successors of *Music and Movement* were called *Movement and Music*, and later *Movement, Mime and Music* (Taylor, 1979, 69).

3.3 Herbert Wiseman and Singing Together

A programme which surpassed all the other music programmes in popularity was *Singing Together*. Herbert Wiseman, the originator of the series, recorded some reminiscences in 1962, about the beginnings:

> The date was September 1939, the BBC had all its preparations made for the autumn term's broadcasts - pamphlets were printed for all subjects, including the music lessons ... Then came the war, and mass evacuation of children from their homes and schools. They were scattered about the country in small detached groups. The issue of pamphlets was stopped, no systematic class instruction was possible, education had to become an affair of hasty improvisation to meet the new enforced conditions. Then somebody had a brainwave. The children were scattered but even when only two or three were gathered together they could still sing. What about broadcasting a few songs and encouraging all, no matter where they were, to take part. A title for such a series? Oh, easy! Singing Together. And on the 25th of September, a few days after the war had begun, we started the series which has gone on till today. ((T) *Scottish Life and Letters* broadcast, 31 December 1962, BBC Sound Archive)

The participants were a few male volunteers from the BBC staff in Glasgow, under the direction of Wiseman. The first broadcast consisted of 'Billy Boy', 'Golden Slumbers' and 'Michael Finnegan', and this set the pattern:

> the first, a 'song with a chorus' which could easily be picked up; the second a 'lovely' tune; and the third 'a little bit of fun'. (Wiseman, 1967, 90)

Soon the *ad hoc* choir was replaced by 'a team of lusty male voices chosen because they were singing at a different pitch from the children' ((T) *Scottish Life and Letters*).

School music teachers working in extremely difficult wartime circumstances were grateful for the programme's unaffected cheerfulness which provided 'love of music by infection and not by injection' (*Music in Schools*, April 1940, 45). It was useful not only in class time but during the long 'black-out' evenings. Pupils recollected and spontaneously sang the songs on country rambles (ibid.). G. Kirkham Jones declared 'let us forget our troubles and join heartily with Herbert Wiseman in Community Singing every Monday morning at 11.00' (*Music in Schools*, November 1939, 253).

It was a programme that was not only enjoyed by schoolchildren of all ages but also 'by mothers, who I'm afraid deserted the Monday wash-tubs to join with us in song' (Wiseman, 1967, 89-90). The repertoire, Wiseman recollected, was extensive and included nursery rhymes, folk songs of different nations, sea shanties, nonsense songs and songs of the Great Masters.

The programme was an instant success. Its listening figures far outstripped those of other school music broadcasts. For example in 1941, Autumn Term, 4100 schools were tuning in: its nearest competitor was *Music and Movement* with 1850 schools. The music programme sub-committee noted:

> the broadcasts are definitely successful in encouraging a community spirit and in getting boys to join in who might not do so in an ordinary singing class. (4 March 1942, Music File 1, 1936-1946, BBC Written Archives)

It also took seriously the criticism that the programme lowered the tone quality of children singing, and requested that broadcasters encourage high quality without destroying the programme's joyousness (ibid.). Although the committee appreciated the popularity of *Singing Together*, the secretary of the Scottish Committee looked upon it as part of a short-term policy, and as interest in music increased, teachers would then take other programmes such as *Rhythm and Melody*, which dealt with aspects of rudiments.

But these other programmes, according to Joseph Smith, found it hard to attract audiences. *Singing Together* was popular because the teachers (in rural schools) 'think it approximated most nearly to their musical needs' (ibid., 3 October 1944). Smith warmed to his theme. To the average teacher, music in school meant songs or hymns, and singing was the only musical activity. Sight reading and aural tests were considered dull and tiresome, and difficult with 40 children in a class. All this highlighted a gap between the attitudes of the average teacher of music, and that of the music programme sub-committee, which wanted to make children curious about music, and to develop a desire to make it.

3.4 Critical Reaction

Finally in this discussion of BBC School Broadcasts let us turn to critical reaction from the musical press. In his regular column 'The School Radio', which appeared in *Music in Schools*, W. R. Anderson constantly drew parallels with similar work in the USA. He was impressed by the work of Walter Damrosch and his *Music Appreciation Hour* on NBC, and by Joseph Maddy whose programme *The Home Symphony* provided elementary instruction in the playing of instruments. Anderson suggested:

> The BBC might consider, with our music teachers, whether some part of the American plan might be beneficial here ... there are developments in the class teaching of instruments ... that might seem worth attention in the light of American experiments. (*Music in Schools*, March-April 1938, 30)

He outlined other possibilities: exchanging reports of musical progress in schools; listening to school orchestras. In other words, what was needed was a greater variety of forms and attacks.

The Musical Times slated school music broadcasts as 'merely disembodied reproductions of an orthodox classroom lesson. Ridiculous! ... The BBC must supplement the normal school lesson, not supersede them' (April 1941, 133-4).

It was clear there were serious doubts about the exact purposes of broadcast music lessons. Dale (1941) carried out a piece of formal research into the broadcasts' pedagogical effectiveness utilising Gibson's Music Appreciation Ability Test No. 2. He set out to compare a group of pupils taking the broadcast *Senior Music Lessons* with a control group of the same standard which was taught the material by a teacher. Both groups used the BBC pamphlets, and the control group had recourse to gramophone records for illustration. In the understanding of musical form, the control group was considered superior. Classroom observation confirmed this: pupils failed to grasp the broadcaster's meaning, showed a distinct lack of interest and failed to concentrate. As far as notation was concerned the control group was clearly superior; notation was a waste of time in broadcasting terms. Although sight singing was not tested, observation showed that the wireless group was unsatisfactory in this regard. Only in the identification of instrumental tone did the wireless group do better. Dale found that after three months of listening the wireless group actually suffered a decline in terms of test results. His conclusions were that with non-specialist teachers the lessons may well be valuable. But the broadcasts were too much like school lessons. Dale recommended that they should confine themselves to material that could not be presented in the ordinary classroom. Indeed the theoretical parts would be much more effectively taught by the teacher.

In reading through the press reaction to the broadcasts there is a continual thread of unease about a lack of vision and a reluctance to take risks.

4. Conclusion

To conclude, I shall consider three questions: (1) what new ideas for the teaching of music were disseminated through radio? (2) how successful were the programmes in teaching traditional musical skills? (3) to what extent did Walford Davies change the face of school music?

When we consider the innovations that the school broadcasts made, tune building, in retrospect, had the greatest potential but suffered through a lack of vision on the part of Walford Davies, and subsequently died. There seems to be some agreement that Davies's work had an immediacy about it (Colles (1942, 137), called it 'good journalism'), but it lacked substance. If we focus on his efforts to encourage children to compose, the criticisms expressed by music advisers and others, suggest that he never sufficiently thought out his position regarding such work. His ideas for teaching children and adults melody writing were the same, there was nothing distinctive which built upon children's innate abilities. The prior steps of extemporisation were not thought through, neither was the vexed question of the relation of all this to notation. The seemingly radical idea of children composing, became, like the programmes themselves, increasingly routine and predictable.

More positively the harnessing of music with movement achieved the popularisation of Dalcroze's ideas on a considerable scale, and broke down some barriers between subjects. Community singing was a populist programme and opened the way for a fresh and informal approach to teaching music in the classroom. Both programmes achieved remarkable popularity, but the freshness of their ideas eventually settled into a routine set of formulas, which became for a time the new orthodoxy.

The backbone of programming, the 'bread and butter' broadcasts of *Elementary Music*, and *Junior* and *Senior Music Lessons*, was problematic. Compared with *Singing Together* and *Music and Movement* these programmes dealt with traditional skills dominated by the teaching of rudiments and notation. Radio's ability to do either appeared severely limited.

There was constant criticism about the conventionality of the school music programmes, and serious doubts as to their precise function in relationship with music teachers. More positively the broadcasts were highly influential in helping define for good or ill the nature of musical education. For countless numbers of children the school music broadcasts were their musical education. Indeed, in conjunction with the government *Handbook of Suggestions for Teachers* (Board of Education, 1937) the broadcasts might be seen as a national model for the music curriculum, prefiguring the official Music National Curriculum by over fifty years.

Finally we come to an assessment of the work of the towering musical figure of this period. Between 1922 and 1941 Walford Davies was a pioneer in the utilisation of the radio and gramophone as instruments to change the face of school music. The sheer quantity of his output is staggering. Between 1924-34 he was responsible for 428 broadcast lessons, 75 studio concerts, 27 published pamphlets, and 60 sets of concert notes for use in conjunction with lessons and concerts (Scholes, 1947, 625).

How is this work to be judged? There are doubts about the effectiveness of his teaching. Scholes (ibid.) declared,

Davies was not the genuinely practical teacher he assumed himself to be, attaching too much importance to fanciful ideas and detailed devices, rather than broadly basing his work on a practical working psychology.

Moreover his record as a broadcaster, together with his membership of the BBC Music Advisory Committee, reinforces the impression that Davies had a strong mission to counter modern influences in whichever sphere he was working. For the teaching of music in schools this could be disastrous, increasing the potential for alienation on the part of the pupils.

However if we develop the idea at the heart of this book that a consideration of music education should not be confined to formal institutional settings, we may find that Davies's work in particular has deeper resonances. At its core was a search for fellowship. In his discussion of the Edwardian temperament, Jonathan Rose (1984) points out that to some Edwardians the discovery of radio waves, with the linking of light to electricity, suggested a vision of universal oneness. We can connect here Wells's notion of 'the schooling of the world' with Davies's understanding of melody as 'the natural language of everybody all the world over' and of the pentatonic scale as 'the scale of the world'. Such thinking prompted some to work for an 'Organic' community, with fellowship at its core. Recovering this sense of community was something that the new mass media could achieve, particularly in alliance with the arts. Scannell and Cardiff (1991) point out that the BBC was perhaps the central agent of the national culture. People could be put in touch with the symbols of a corporate national life, a common culture, through access to the arts. It is in this context that Davies influenced national musical life immeasurably through recording and broadcasting. More specifically he linked the Gramophone Company and the BBC to the practical concerns of the teaching and learning of music in schools and the community.

Whereas Davies's work with the new media did not change the face of school music as he had hoped - it was too flawed for that - his contribution must be seen within this overall wider vision of the fellowship of music, which extended from soldiers' barrack rooms to active holiday ventures, to schools, to churches, and to the fireside listener. It is in this attempt to connect different musical worlds that Walford Davies has the most to say to us.

4 Musical Education of the Under-Twelves 1949-1983

The aim of this chapter is to chart the progress of the Musical Education of the Under-Twelves (MEUT) Association which linked pre-war to post-war concerns within music education, and developed them further. Although not established until 1949, it arose, as I shall demonstrate, from a coalition of a number of pre-war societies and associations, and until its demise in 1983 played a part in the development of primary school music education. The history of such an association provides a valuable lens through which we can identify underlying patterns of change and conflict within a subject, and in the process provide the 'local detail' which influenced the development of music education in the primary school, and later in the middle school, over more than thirty years (see Goodson, 1988).

I shall consider the following questions: what were the diverse historical roots of MEUT? Why was MEUT formed? What new ideas were developed and debated? How did these new ideas relate to traditional concerns? What accounted for the demise of MEUT?

But first I will chart the general development of music education in primary schools from 1949 until 1972. The rest of this story will be dealt with in the next chapter, dealing as it does with music education into the late 1970s, including a major Schools Council project dealing with primary school music.

1. Music in Primary Schools 1949-1972

In 1933 the Board of Education published a highly optimistic report entitled *Recent Developments in School Music* (Board of Education, 1933). The class teacher of music was suffering from an *embarras de richesses*. The diverse activities were itemised with pride: appreciation of music, community singing, concerts, country dancing, festivals, the gramophone, the school orchestra, pianoforte classes, pipe making and playing, rhythmic work and wireless lessons. Moreover, music lessons in the opinion of the report's authors had played a great part in the gradual transformation of musical life in England since the nineteenth century.

Seventeen years later, Percy Smith writing in the journal *Music in Education* (1950) bemoaned the fact that nothing of substance for music teachers had been published to rival the 1937 *Handbook of Suggestions for Teachers* (Board of Education, 1937). That volume had in his opinion developed views about the place of music in education, and had collated experience gained from the teaching of it. But now teachers were in a new context shaped by the 1944 Education Act (see Lowe, 1988, Part One). To emphasise the urgency of the matter he drew attention to a Ministry of Education pamphlet called *Story of a School* (Stone, 1949). In it the former headmaster of a junior school chronicled his work, particularly in the creative arts. Movement and mime are given prominence. Smith relates 'As the story unfolds one looks forward with eagerness for the part music played in the scheme. A jolt comes. A chapter is headed "Music and Arithmetic". This seems a curious alliance' (ibid., 166). It transpires that in spite of Stone giving more thought to the development of music than anything else, he had had to bracket it with maths 'because in each we failed to find an approach which allowed all the children to find complete absorption' (ibid., 29). He did try to encourage the children to compose tunes for dramatic work, but it became laborious and he had to fall back on conventional methods. Singing at sight and reading music he found too intellectual for the children. Finally he asked the question: 'was the failure due to an interpretative approach without giving the child an experience of it as a creative art?' All this led Smith to reiterate the need for substantial guidance for music teachers, so they could at least enter the debate about whether music education could be truly creative.

These publications illustrate something of the evolution of concerns between pre-war and post-war practice in music education, from music making based upon group performance, an interpretative approach, towards one focusing upon individual invention.

Smith had to wait until 1956, for the first edition of *Music in Schools* published by the Ministry of Education. It recommended that nursery and infant pupils be encouraged to experiment with sounds, that there need be no formal instruction as that was out of step with the ideals of modern classrooms. The more freely music entered the daily life of small children the better. The music corner should contain a variety of good quality instruments such as tambourines, xylophones etc. so that the pupils learned at first-hand about pitch relations, tone quality, differences in volume. Percussion instruments used imaginatively could be combined effectively with dramatic work and singing. The message was drummed home:

> In all instrumental work the small group is preferable to the large class; indeed the conventional 'percussion band lesson' might give place to more flexible treatment in which small groups of players form only part of a varied pattern that can include singing and movement. (Ibid., 14)

Movement in the curriculum required clear thinking and continued study.

Children could supply their own music to dance to, utilising percussion instruments to work out their own rhythmic patterns: they might even produce their own scorings. Certainly creative work was possible through the interaction of instruments, singing and movement. Pupils were known to enjoy improvising plays and ballad operas. There is an intriguing resonance with future developments in the National Curriculum in the report's observation that the tape recorder was a useful aid enabling children to 'appraise' their own compositions at an early stage. But the document offered a word of caution:

> There is as yet little evidence to show sustained development in children's power to make up their own tunes ... We do not yet know how many children are capable of pursuing this kind of creativeness to a point of achievement and satisfaction. (Ibid., 19-20)

As far as staffing was concerned the report was clear in its preference:

> In any school where there is the desire to let music play its part in an integrated scheme of junior education, free from excessive time-table domination, some parts at least of the teaching must fall to the class teacher. (Ibid., 16)

In its final comments, *Music in Schools* welcomed opportunities for collaboration with other subjects.

A second edition of the publication appeared in 1969, and a comparison is illuminating. It acknowledged the notable developments that had taken place in creative music making, instrumental playing, and assessment. Yet the report admitted that music inside schools had changed less than on the outside.

The hesitation about tune making expressed in the first edition was abandoned. Children could start with a restricted choice of notes rather as Carl Orff advocated, and later would become adventurous and use additional notes in improvisation:'one of the chief functions of the resourceful teacher is to open the pupils' eyes to the possibilities that lie open before them' (ibid., 13).

There is still a note of caution. It was argued that unlike the other arts, music was largely re-creative, and in the past this element received most of the attention. But in the end the emphasis had to rely upon the teacher's discretion: 'he must decide how much attention he should give to teaching musical skills ... and how much he should reserve for the joys of creating or re-creating music' (ibid., 20). This endorsement of teacher freedom might also be read as an expression of uncertainty and agnosticism about the creative possibilities of music education.

All these doubts were apparently swept aside with the publication in 1970 of a DES (Department of Education and Science) Report in Education entitled

Creative Music in Education (DES, 1970). Developed by a small group of HMI, it serves as an account of some of the ways in which creative music was being developed in primary and secondary schools. In its preamble it noted that through the increased availability of good quality classroom instruments 'which facilitate progress without undue preoccupation with technique' (ibid., 1) children were now able to work with the raw materials of the musician, just as those of the poet and artist.

The report examined creative music making from two aspects: through experiment children may discover the nature of sounds and improvise their own music, either individually or in groups; or they may take an existing melody and make an arrangement of it for voices and instruments.

A developmental approach was advocated. Children of pre-school age readily experiment with sounds, banging a spoon or kitchen utensils. At school they need a variety of instruments, either in the classroom, or in a special music corner. Five year olds gradually begin to distinguish between the various properties of the instruments, they discover a rhythm or melody that pleases, they gradually acquire mastery. As children develop socially they show an inclination towards working in groups. They adjust to one another's ideas, they copy motifs. There is no need at this stage, the report continued, to use a definite scale plan. The sounds may appear strange to adults, but children gradually evolve an instinctive feeling for balance and texture. At this stage the pentatonic scale, the basis of so much of the world's music, comes into its own. At first such work can be purely improvisatory. Simple musical ideas can be developed through exploring differences in timbre, speed and pitch.

Suitable stimuli are suggested: Noah's Journey, David and Goliath, Yorkshire Caves, Canterbury Pilgrims. Children can invent their own notation, a graphic like score. The teacher can help the child by writing out its tune. Admittedly the role of the teacher is problematic. She must know when to prompt, when to withdraw. But essentially it is the quality of relationships within the classroom which will lead to the most satisfying work. The report concluded:

> It is difficult to forecast the future of music education in this country. Certainly few would now dispute the view that the solely passive approach is doomed to failure ... Through creative music it becomes possible for a majority of pupils of all ages and abilities to experience the deep satisfaction of participation. (Ibid., 4)

The gist of this report was amplified in John Horton's (1972) book on music in the primary school which was significant because it was part of a series documenting progressive ideas, published by the Schools Council. But we can also read it, bearing in mind Horton's recent retirement as HMI with responsibility for music, as a quasi-official view. Significantly he does acknowledge the help of his colleagues within the inspectorate who chose suitable recordings of work in the classroom.

In particular Horton has interesting things to say concerning the development of instrumental and creative work. After being somewhat critical of the percussion band movement because it was frequently aesthetically unsatisfying, he points out that now instruments could be distributed to music corners and activity groups with the accent on discovery. Horton observes that the Orff method had consolidated much of the practice in primary schools over twenty years. It underlined the importance of the creative aspect of music education, in which field 'some of the most revolutionary advances have been taking place' (ibid., 15).

Horton noted that dance and drama had been the first arts subjects to break away from the domination of performance to assert the claims of the individual imagination. The visual arts followed with Marion Richardson in the 1920s. In music however there have been two modes of creativity - the composer and performer. We had until now favoured the latter. But Horton reckoned that creativeness had won general (although not universal) acceptance. What was new about the book was that it was accompanied by a disc of tape-recorded compositions from a variety of classrooms.

These ideas were all very well, but what happened in practice? We can draw upon three reports which investigated aspects of music in primary schools. The School Broadcasting Council prepared a draft report on *Music in Junior School* (c1953). It noted that in practice music in such schools basically consisted of singing. The average weekly provision for the subject was 60-80 minutes, and there were many schools that relied completely on the radio for the teaching. The report lamented how much better it would be if the programmes acted as a supplement instead. The problem was that it proved difficult to find out what constituted a music course. No syllabus was laid down by local authorities: it was impossible to prescribe a minimum standard of attainment, because the quality of teachers was so variable. In one school the children observed were

> unmistakably musical, but they are music starved because the teacher cannot and will not attempt to teach them anything independently or even to follow up the broadcasts. In all other subjects she is most competent! (Ibid., 4)

The report acknowledged that training colleges did their best with 'basic' or 'background' courses, but the musical calibre of the students was very low. Many students probably hoped that they could get by without having to teach music.

The BBC report focused upon three programmes, *Time and Tune*, *Rhythm and Melody*, and *Singing Together*. The main constituents of the first two of these series comprised songs, rhythm and notation teaching, experience of orchestral instruments and music for listening. The following comments from a teacher were taken as representative of the impression made on many, and in the light of the previous chapter we note some similarities:

> Mr X thought today's broadcast was fairly typical of the series as a whole, and wondered whether Miss Whitbread was not trying to do too much in dealing with so many aspects of music. He thought himself that the really important parts were the teaching of songs, the rhythm names, and the beating of the rhythms by the class and the musical appreciation. He thought that much of what she did in the realm of notation belonged to a later sphere of school work. The reason that he took the broadcasts himself was that he could expect no specialist help and he looked to Miss Whitbread for this. It was most important to him that the broadcasts should not attempt less than he could do, nor more than a majority of the chldren could hope to do, and he suspected that at present the broadcasts were erring on the latter side rather than on the former. (Ibid., 12-13)

Singing Together was still the most popular of the music broadcasts. There was talk of trying to extend its scope, but Bernard Shore, the HM Staff Inspector for Music, expressed the general feeling that

> We've got to be realistic - it's a compromise whatever is done. The point is that with what the BBC is doing now, the teacher can prepare the lesson, you get the children to look at the staff notation, and they learn more songs. People with no facilities get something, others can use the broadcasts more fully. (Ibid., 15)

The pessimistic conclusion of the BBC report however was that progress in rectifying the unsatisfactory nature of music in primary schools would be very slow.

Certainly as far as the training of music teachers was concerned, the Report by the Standing Conference of Music Committees (1954) agreed with much of the substance of the BBC's observations. Training and recruitment remained in an unsatisfactory state. Perhaps in the majority of publicly maintained schools, it was estimated, music was taught inadequately. The number of teachers able to teach music in primary schools was insufficient, and training colleges had done too little in the past: 'The need for action is urgent' (ibid., 3).

A survey published by the Schools' Music Association in 1961 identified as a key weakness the shortage of music teachers to teach in primary schools. A head teacher observed that '99 per cent of applicants for posts say 'no' to music' (ibid., 2). In the 912 schools that replied to the request for information it was reckoned that 52 per cent of teachers actually taught some music. But only a minority included any music reading in their teaching. Moreover in a large number of cases, classes combined for music, which mostly consisted of singing. One respondent wrote:

Judging from the popularity of *6.5 Special, DrumBeat* and *Juke Box Jury,* the choral singing which is the only music experienced by the majority of the children fails completely to register or have any impact on the emotional lives of the children. I think it is too passive - the best work is done when the music is allied to dancing or done as instrumental work. (Ibid., 4)

The report was not all unrelieved gloom however. There was work developing with percussion instruments, Carl Orff was mentioned, as well as tonic sol-fa, French time names and bamboo pipes and recorders. Music was welcomed by some as a break from academic subjects, one reply stated it was the one subject enjoyed by both teacher and children. Difficult children were often found to improve their attitude after learning the recorder. When something unhappy occurred in the classroom, music was the quickest way to restore the peace.

Thus we see in this picture of music in primary schools an uneasy mix of high ideals, pragmatic solutions, and under-achievement. With this perspective in view I shall now focus upon the attempts of a subject association to renew and revitalise the subject in the post-war era.

2. Musical Education of the Under-Twelves (MEUT)

At a meeting of the Percussion Band Association in 1947, the view was expressed 'that it was most desirable that not only all the branches of musical training be coordinated, but that there should also be coordination with the general mental and physical development of the child' (Chairman's Report, n.d., MEUT Minutes). It was agreed that a meeting should be called of all those interested. This was subsequently held at the Cora Hotel in London, and it was followed by two informal meetings, one at the home of Leslie Regan and the other at the Royal Academy of Music. An executive committee was formed. The original members were: Yvonne Adair (a percussion band specialist), Kathleen Blocksidge and Gladys Helliwell (both lecturers in music at Philippa Fawcett Training College), Winifred Houghton (lecturer in music, Gipsy Hill Training College), Gwendoline Skett (lecturer in music, Rachel McMillan Training College), Elizabeth Barnard (lecturer in music, Goldsmith's College). There were three co-opted members, Philip Pfaff (Music Organiser, East Ham Education Committee) and Leslie Welton (from the publishers, Joseph Williams), and Florence James. The overwhelming influence of training colleges is apparent, and these colleges were within the federation of the London University Institute of Education.

Between 50 and 60 people attended a public meeting at the Waldegrave Hall, London on 26 February 1949, approved the title Musical Education of the Under-Twelves, and adopted its proposed aims and objects (MEUT Constitution, n.d., MEUT Minutes):

- To stress the importance of music in the general education of the child.
- To promote more efficient musical training in the schools by co-ordinating all the existing musical activities.
- To organise discussion conferences and lecture courses at which teachers may receive guidance from specialists.
- To affirm the value of music in the development of the child's whole personality.
- To undertake any other musical activities considered necessary.

Kathleen Blocksidge, the driving force and the instigator of the Association outlined the thinking of the members of the initial group who had formulated the ideas. Although the foundations of music training needed to start with very young children, in many schools music work was unbalanced and unco-ordinated. This was partly due to the insufficient training afforded classroom teachers, many of whom supplemented it by attending courses. The problem, however, was that such teachers tended to concentrate on one element of the musical menu, for example the percussion band, pipe playing, or eurhythmics. It was one of the purposes of the association to help provide a balanced musical diet, so that children could move, sing, play music and read it, and come to know the literature of music. For her, the association needed to act in an advisory capacity to teachers, to issue a regular bulletin, and to form a committee comprising the various associations which made up MEUT (Address by K. Blocksidge, February 1949, MEUT Minutes).

At the inaugural meeting it was announced that Ernest Read, the distinguished musician and Dalcroze-influenced educator had accepted the invitation to become president of the association, that there was an intention to form an advisory council, and that the following societies and institutions had expressed their support: the University of London, Institute of Education; the National Froebel Foundation; the Nursery School Association; the Percussion Band Association; The Dalcroze Society; the Pipers' Guild; the Bow-Craft Guild (ibid.). It was these groups that comprised the kernel of the association's life, in addition to the Recorder Society which joined at a later date.

At this point we need to pause to consider the significance of the different elements that comprised this cluster of musical and educational interests. The University of London Institute of Education was the Area Training Organisation within which the London training colleges operated (Dent, 1977, 116-7). The National Froebel Foundation, formed in 1938, represented a vital strand of the thinking of the leading members of the association (see Woodham-Smith, 1952). Music had always formed an important part of Froebelian philosophy, ranging from Froebel's *Mother's Songs, Games and Stories* (1907 (1843)), to Eleanore Heerwart's publication for English schools, *Music for the Kindergarten* (1877). We shall see later that two eminent Froebelians,

Evelyn Lawrence and Molly Brearley had some significant involvement with the association.

The equally influential Nursery School Association had been formed in 1923 with Margaret McMillan as its first president. It aimed to persuade local authorities to open nursery schools and classes. McMillan herself had studied music in Germany, and remained convinced that the human voice was the primary sense in social organisation. She discussed music both in terms of a hunger, 'a felt need on the child's part', and as an innate capacity (Steedman, 1990, 220). The Nursery School Association propagandised through the extensive publication of leaflets and pamphlets, to which Kathleen Blocksidge contributed (Blocksidge, 1957).

The longest established of the musical organisations comprising MEUT was the Dalcroze Society formed in 1915 (see Tingey, 1980). It stemmed from the visit to England by Jaques-Dalcroze in 1912. Dalcroze (1865-1950) believed firmly in the unity of music and rhythmic movement, which he developed into the practice of eurhythmics. He was convinced that the most natural response to rhythm must be through a total muscular and nervous bodily reaction. Dalcroze devised a series of graded exercises which encouraged pupils to react physically to musical rhythm (see Dobbs, 1976, and Jaques-Dalcroze, 1967). The links with Dalcroze were apparent within the association. Ernest Read had been an early devoted disciple, and from 1919-1939 was Director of the London School of Dalcroze Eurhythmics, becoming chairman of the Dalcroze Society from 1947-1965 (see Zagni, 1989). He was succeeded in this function by another President of MEUT, Reginald Rennoldson. But it was one of the association's key members, Winifred Houghton who perhaps had the most crucial role in disseminating Dalcroze's ideas. She had studied with him, became Warden of the Dalcroze Centre in 1949, and wrote several books on the Dalcroze method (Houghton, 1951, 1957).

The Pipers' Guild had been established by Margaret James in 1932, based upon work carried out from 1926 at Findlay Street School, Fulham in 1926 (James, 1932). The aims of the society were Ruskinian in scope and expression. Over-specialisation and machinery had excluded Everyman from an active share in the arts. But, James argued, such arts as handicraft, design and music making are natural, universal capacities which belong to Everyman. She had first encountered pipe music in Sicily, and came to realise its place in the heritage of European peasantry. Its educational implications were clear to her. Central to her educational thinking was an emphasis upon cross-disciplinary work: children had to make, decorate and play their instruments. Significantly in view of later developments James believed: 'when the music, craft and art teachers are determined to combine their efforts to bring about a hand-made orchestra, there will be creative music in schools' (ibid., 8). The Guild not only spread to schools, but established itself amongst adults in England and abroad.

The most fervent follower of James' work was Kathleen Blocksidge, who developed the ideals in her early publication combining pipe and percussion bands (1934). Significantly Margaret James contributed a foreword which planted the idea in Blocksidge's mind that was to become MEUT: 'A spirit which is ready to co-ordinate the good in various methods is lacking. We need unity in our work' (ibid., iii). Blocksidge later developed a reputation for the making of musical apparatus in schools (Blocksidge, 1957).

The Bow-Craft Guild had been established in 1937 and organised by Leonard Welton, himself a co-opted member of the MEUT committee (Bow-Craft Guild, 1948). Originally the Guild set out to develop string teaching but expanded to encompass the formation of junior orchestras. By 1948 its aims were 'to provide a complete and co-ordinated Scheme for the Development of Instrumental Music in Schools by means of Violin Classes, leading to the School Orchestra: embracing also the early stages of Rhythmic and Melodic Training through Percussion Band and Recorder Classes' (ibid., 1). The Guild, about which there is little information, was closely associated with the music publisher, Joseph Williams, and one of the pioneers of instrumental music teaching, John Hullah Brown (see Hullah Brown, 1938). Ernest Read was listed as an early supporter.

As we have seen the initial impetus for the forming of MEUT came from the Percussion Band Association. This had been formed in 1939 (Southcott, 1992), but it had a much longer history, going back to the work of Marie Salt at Streatham High School in 1909 (MacPherson and Read, 1912), and to the kindergarten band, one of the earliest features of the kindergarten (Woodham-Smith, 1952, 73). Both Kathleen Blocksidge and Yvonne Adair became involved in percussion bands through an early pioneer, Louie de Rusette (see Rainbow Correspondence: K. Blocksidge to Bernarr Rainbow 1 March, 1970). But it was Adair who was to become one of the driving forces behind the development of the movement after the war, particularly through her writing and arranging (Adair, 1952). Percussion bands were commonly found in pre-war schools: children played their defined parts on drums, tambourines and triangles, whilst a pianist supplied the melodic and harmonic texture. A key feature was the use of child conductors.

It was this cluster of societies that gave a continuity to the work of the Association, in dealing with new ideas and methods that inevitably developed in post-war education. Yet it is noticeable that they possessed very different aims and methodologies, difficult in practice to combine.

At this point I return to the development of MEUT, which soon established a pattern of activity which would persist for the rest of its life. Every year there were two conferences, which generally took place in London. Many of these would include 'lecture-demonstrations' utilising school choirs and orchestras to illustrate practical teaching points. Typical themes were 'The Place of Music in the Junior School', 'Music Broadcasts in the Classroom',

'The Integration of Music with Activities' etc. There were occasional calls for the association to spread its wings, and indeed it did hold a couple of meetings in Luton and Winchester, but its finances were severely stretched by such outings.

In addition MEUT published a modest cyclostyled Bulletin twice a year, which contained summaries of the conference papers, book reviews and the occasional special article. The membership of the Association was always fairly small, starting off at its launch with 148, and generally hovering until its final years, around the 100 mark.

In its pioneering days MEUT tried to weave itself 'into the web of musical education in this country' (24 February 1951, MEUT Minutes), in the process keeping a watch on other bodies. It set up a panel of approved lecturers and a list of schools where good teaching could be observed (ibid., 18 November 1950). It was keen also to liaise with the British Council to show foreign visitors examples of good practice in English music education. In December 1952 it had contributed a session to the 36th Annual Conference of Educational Associations at King's College London, where it staged demonstrations on musical activity in the Infant School, music through movement, and combined music making with percussion band, singing and instrumental work. One of its early achievements was the organising of a Coronation Concert in May 1953 at St Martin-in-the-Fields, at which a massed choir from six London schools took part, in addition to a bamboo pipe band.

Ernest Read's successor as president in 1965 was Jack Dobbs, a lecturer at the Central College of the London University Institute of Education and co-author of the influential *Oxford School Music Books* series (Fiske and Dobbs, 1954-61; Dobbs and Firth, 1959). His presidential address was entitled significantly 'New aspects on Music Teaching'. By now the Plowden Report was in the air, and it seemed to engender a new feeling of optimism in the Association. In 1968 MEUT organised with the Pipers' Guild the 5th Joint Music in Schools conference. In the *Music Teacher* report (December 1968 in MEUT Minutes) it was observed that 'with MEUT a joint host, it was not surprising that the emphasis should be on creative work by younger age-groups'. An Infant School class sang folk songs incorporating movement and craft, two junior schools demonstrated group work. *Music Teacher* commented 'with obvious enjoyment they made music on pitched percussion, and created sound effects to illustrate their own stories (although one could not help wondering whether the latter could strictly be called music)' (ibid.). Bamboo pipes were in evidence too, as well as a brass and woodwind demonstration, and a massed choir.

At the AGM in 1966 it was noted with enthusiasm that the previous year could be associated with the word 'increase'. In the following year's Spring conference, for the first time, people had to be turned away. By 1968 members were being urged to fight complacency: 'we must not be content with our signs of growth but press on to enlarge the membership and one of the ways was for young people to share in the running of the society' (16 March 1968, MEUT Minutes).

In 1972 Jack Dobbs resigned as president due to his new post at Dartington College of Arts. His successor was Reginald Rennoldson, Music Inspector for the Inner London Education Authority (ILEA). On his death two years later, the writer, composer and educator Geoffrey Winters became the Association's final president. The 'seventies were difficult years for the Association. In the minutes one reads that the 'flu epidemic in 1970 had caused a deficit at the conference, the following year the conference and AGM had had to be postponed due to the postal strike, and in 1974 the train strike had made for conference planning problems.

In 1975 the Association took the significant step of extending membership to teachers in middle schools. The name Musical Education Up to Thirteen, enabled the acronym still to be used. This extension of membership had been discussed right throughout the association's history, as early as March 1955. But now it had added urgency, as a source for further recruitment.

But in spite of this new constrained atmosphere the association was developing new ideas, coming to terms with fresh challenges. There were sessions on the steel band, on electronic music, and on creative music in secondary schools. Elizabeth Barnard reiterated the association's progressive remit: 'MEUT provides a platform for more challenging and experimental work than is offered elsewhere' (19 May 1973, MEUT Minutes).

However the future looked bleak. By 1973 only one of the original sponsoring organisations, the Pipers' Guild, was paying an annual subscription (9 May 1973, MEUT Minutes). The attitude of teachers towards courses had changed: 'some thought Saturdays should be a time when they could forget school. More authorities were giving In-service courses' (19 May 1973, MEUT Minutes).

The years coincided with the widespread closure, amalgamation and restructuring of Colleges of Education (see Dent, 1977, chap. 24). In the September 1976 Bulletin there was a valedictory air:

> I offer my sympathy to the staff of the many Colleges of Education which face possible closures. A number have excellent music departments giving future class teachers the opportunity to further their musical talents and to give those who think they are not musically gifted, confidence to take music with their classes. (MEUT *Bulletin*, February 1977, 1)

A decline in membership was associated with the taking over by local education authorities of in-service training, as well as the reduction in the number of music students in colleges of education.

By the end of the decade there was talk of having to reconsider the association's role (1 February 1979, MEUT Minutes). There were clearly new priorities to come to terms with. John Stephens, music inspector for ILEA, and a former HMI, talked of the pressure on music from expanding subject areas (MEUT *Bulletin*, January 1978). Music teachers had to be able to justify music's place primarily for what it could do for children that other subjects could not. Stephens quoted Roy Jenkins' notion of 'equal opportunities with cultural diversity in an atmosphere of tolerance' (ibid.). Music educators, Stephens continued, had to tackle the ethnic influences which prevailed in inner city schools, and ask what could be learnt from other cultures. Technology provided young people with immediate access to music, they may not even need a teacher.

The low-point was reached in December 1980, when only 25 attended the conference. Kathleen Blocksidge spoke for the closure of the association, despite her feelings of great sadness (14 March 1981, MEUT Minutes). There was some effort made to transfer the association to the Schools' Music Association, but the offer was rejected due to the present climate of financial and administrative restrictions. Instead the funds were transferred to the University of Reading in connection with its in-service work for music teachers. The minute books and bulletins were also deposited there. These archival documents have served as my principle sources of evidence. They have defined my enquiry, and the theory is grounded in the material I have unearthed.

In this account I have attempted to provide an overview of the antecedents of the Association, its founding, and its rise and fall. Next I shall examine its ideas and practice.

3. The Progressive Ideal and Musical Creativity

Right from the establishment of MEUT there was an alignment with progressive educational ideas, probably stemming from the fact that Blocksidge and her committee were predominantly working within teacher training colleges, which at least up until the war had acted as one of the agents of progressivism (see Cunningham, 1988). Cunningham has identified the main traits of progressivism as: reduction in teacher authoritarianism; alternatives to class lessons; dissolution of the formal timetable; a shift from the 3 R's to more creative and expressive activities. Underlying all this was a belief in individuality, freedom and growth.

The opening conference of the Association on 1st July 1949 developed a vision of the way music in primary schools could move forward. The keynote speaker was Dr Evelyn Lawrence, Director of the National Froebel Foundation. She wondered how music education was coping with the current vogue for 'free methods of general education' (MEUT *Bulletin*, September 1949). More directly she asked: what are your techniques in fitting in music into a free curriculum? Do music teachers want a specific place on the timetable, or do they want to be musical advisers in a school where the timetable is mainly a free one with the children choosing their own jobs at their own time?

She believed that if a great deal of music making materials were distributed, children would create their own tunes and rhythms and thus lay a foundation for appreciating the music of others. This creative impulse could be guided. Once they had gained the habit of making pleasant noises and pleasant rhythms with the apparatus provided, they would soon want to write them down and record what they have done. Lawrence's speech provided an identification with progressive ideas, a way forward from a preoccupation with massed percussion playing and singing.

This emphasis upon spontaneity was developed by the psychologist and teacher trainer, P.M. Pickard of the Froebel Educational Institute (see Pickard 1970). She identified as one of the most startling of recent discoveries the connection of the play of the child and the creativity of the artist:

> It was not until the psychoanalytical approach could be brought to mind that it was realised, first, that the fantasies of the children at play bear a remarkable resemblance to the fantasies of the artist at work ... both are distancing and proportioning experiences of very great intensity. (MEUT *Bulletin*, June 1952, 4)

It was no surprise to her that there were three sections of the population which refused to close the lid on living: infants, adolescents and artists.

The centrality of the child's present experience was underlined by Molly Brearley, the principal of the Froebel Institute, a member of the Plowden Committee, identified by Cunningham (1988) as a liberal romantic. She addressed the question 'Why Teach Music?' asking uncomfortably, why after having many hours devoted to it in their school lives, do children eventually react against music? (MEUT *Bulletin,* June 1957). Brearley believed that too much attention in the past had been addressed to the child's future needs. We have to relate to the child's development now. But we also have to foster values other than the material ones.

The subjectivity of music, she believed, was its strength. It extended the range of delicacy of children's feelings by evocation, rather than description. Its subjectivity made it distinctive. Children were able to nourish themselves upon it. Whilst music possessed an undoubted intellectual content Brearley warned that musical theory had to grow out of practice:

> If you have to resort to notes dwelling in houses, fairies or birds sitting on fences or telegraph wires, you are attempting to train past understanding ... I madden my musical friends by saying that I believe that in fifty years' time sol-fa and ta-te will be dead. (Ibid., 9)

But she believed that music's greatest contribution was to spiritual development. Admittedly this was difficult to talk about. She quoted Carlyle on music, as 'unfathomable speech which takes us to the edge of the infinite and lets us for moments gaze upon that' (ibid., 10). With such an aim, enjoyment was a bonus. Essentially music was able to combat incuria and indifference, the biggest enemies of the spirit. Music seldom gave children wrong impressions in the way that words could.

In all of this we notice a rhetoric in tune with progressivism, dealing with individual needs and present experience. But how might the rhetoric be matched in practice? This was the task of the Association. Jack Dobbs developed these ideas in relation to music teaching in his presidential address to the Association (MEUT *Bulletin*, September 1966). He argued that until recently the teaching of music had been focused on the group, as in the choral society and the orchestra. These were essentially voluntary in nature, and dependent upon a leader. Often the passivity of members of the group lay unnoticed until the leader was absent. The music classroom however was compulsory. This gave rise to different problems. Dobbs noted that in other curriculum areas like physical education and art, teachers had developed skills which released the natural process. Music educators needed to take note. But he did not minimise the scale of the problem of adapting to a new way of thinking. There were subject-related problems that made progress difficult, particularly noise levels. But he noted children were oblivious to this and moreover, instruments were now available that meant it was impossible to make an ugly sound.

The important point for Dobbs was to move away from the extremes of viewing the child as an isolated individual or as part of a massed activity, and instead focus upon the interplay of personality upon personality in smaller, informal groups. In such settings children mature emotionally and socially. Music is an activity which lends itself to sharing, between children and the teacher, and the teacher and her class. No longer is the teacher the hander out of information, a trainer of skills or a director of performances. She is a person skilled in the art of creating situations in which the child will want to learn for himself. She must be prepared for her existence to be forgotten. The most successful teacher fires the imagination and stimulates the intellect.

This emphasis upon creativity, Dobbs believed to be crucial. He warned, nevertheless, that it should not be confused with free expression. Our children must be nourished on fantasy, poetry and painting, and all things beautiful and full of wonder. There is a tremendous variety of sounds around us, in isolation and combination. But there is no place for compartmentalisation:

Music is not a subject to be brought out of deep freeze for the lesson and returned there when the bell has gone. It was with the child before lessons began and will be with him in his old age. (Ibid., 5)

In many ways this was a key speech in the history of the Association, heralding a new era: it was in tune with the soon-to-be published Plowden Report, *Children and their Primary Schools* (CACE, 1967) which was a bombshell for music teachers. The report castigated music teaching for its reliance on mass instruction, over-direction by the teacher and a lack of any notion of individual progression. As a creative subject it lagged behind arts and crafts and language.

A year later Doris Flynn (MEUT *Bulletin*, February 1968) extracted and highlighted significant ideas for music educators from Plowden. Of overriding importance was the notion that what children learn is of less importance than what they experience. A musical education would benefit all children only if it made due allowances for their developing attitudes. She selected three principles from the report. First, children need to be known as individuals, and hence have a personal approach to learning. Flynn noted the traditional barriers of the set lessons and the BBC programme schedule. Second, there should be a skilful construction of an educational environment and close integration of children's interest and experience with skills and knowledge. For musicians there needed to be more doors opened, literally and metaphorically, a greater provision of classroom instruments, and a closer concentration on the sounds of nature. Finally, teachers should be encouraged to look at the wholeness of the school day, adjusting particular events to the children's immediate needs.

It was John Paynter who addressed the association in 1970, the same year in which *Sound and Silence* (Paynter and Aston, 1970) was published. In an earlier article in *Music in Education* (Paynter, 1967) he had reacted to Plowden. He pointed out that Herbert Read and Marion Richardson had shown the creative way in art, followed by Peter Slade in drama. The explosion of creative writing in English was the latest manifestation of this revolution. At the Association's conference (MEUT *Bulletin*, October 1971) he noted that we had to start with raw materials, sound and silence. If we become excited by the sounds and use them and symbolise them in patterns, they will become music: 'children must learn to do with what they have' (ibid., 14). Paynter's later work with the Schools Council, as I shall recount in the next chapter, exerted a profound influence on creative music making in secondary schools (see Paynter, 1982).

It was always the intention of the Association to spread good practice breaking away from the domination of specific activities, in order to provide a more coherent philosophy. The development of creative work permeated much of this activity, anticipating Plowden's critique, and extending from it.

For example, Kathleen Blocksidge in the early 'fifties demonstrated how the boys from Aberdour Prep School had arranged their own music for the pipes, written their own tunes, and moreover played them 'with simple naturalness' (MEUT *Bulletin*, January 1951). She observed (MEUT *Bulletin*,

January 1954) that teachers felt anxious about the creative side of music making. But, she argued, as music is the art in which the child can first express himself, surely we could foster spontaneous expression. Two points arose however: spontaneous expression in music making was generally a solitary pursuit; most music needed a level of skill. She reckoned the right environment was the free activity period and breaktimes. The problem for music was that one child liberating its ego musically may disturb the whole class. This is what made the subject different from painting, pottery and literature.

Other demonstrations of creative work in action included: recordings of children from the Park School, Doncaster, in the throes of melodic invention (ibid.); using Laban's ideas in linking movement with the development of musical creativity (MEUT *Bulletin*, July 1960) with children being asked to choose an instrument so as to express the quality of its sound in movement, resulting in paired dance, subjecting the music and dance to the will of the other. In the light of the Plowden Report, Marjorie Glynne-Jones (MEUT *Bulletin*, February 1968) pointed out that when young children enter school they paint quite naturally, they see things we take for granted. Children's music, like their painting, she argued, should be different from that of adults. The conference witnessed demonstrations of children improvising in pairs and trios, with the rest of the class commenting on balance, form, beginnings and endings.

All these examples of good practice stemmed from a child-centred approach, within the parameters of progressive ideas about education. But there were other influences which seemed to take over the thinking about creative work. There was a move away from child centredness in the development of the Orff method, and secondary schools came to dominate the agenda about creativity with an influence derived from the musical avant-garde.

Orff's system brought together elements in music education that had been treated mostly in isolation: solo and choral singing, instrumental teaching, aural training in pitch and time, the combination of words with music and of movement with music, and improvisation. All this within the scope of the majority of pupils (see Horton, 1976; Orff, 1978).

Mention of Carl Orff (1895-1982) and his ideas surfaced at an Association conference in 1962 (MEUT *Bulletin*, September 1962) when Doris Gould spoke of classroom experiments based on his ideas. She demonstrated patterning with words and proverbs, transferring to chime bars and xylophone, based on a minor third. The children could 'doodle' on this, and gradually encompass the pentatonic scale. Creative variations were infinite in their possibilities. Eventually children would want to write their own tunes.

The BBC promulgated Orff's ideas. When John Hosier talked of 'Music through Television for the Primary School' (MEUT *Bulletin*, February 1965) he pointed out that much was based on the 'Orff' approach, teaching rhythm first hand, and developing accompaniments. It is of interest that we hear that William Murphy of the BBC was looking for a development of the long running series *Time and Tune* (MEUT *Bulletin*, February 1967). He was told he could go anywhere in Europe to get new ideas. He attended an Orff course in Salzburg, which he felt too difficult as it stood, he then turned to Kodály (1882-1967) in Hungary. It was Kodály's achievement to develop a method of teaching concerned with the development of the inner ear effected through singing, particularly part singing, before the pupil is introduced to instrumental playing (see Russell-Smith, 1976; Sandor, 1969).

The result of Murphy's researches was a synthesis of the two approaches in the series *Music Workshop*. Certainly although Kodály's and Orff's techniques and philosophies were quite different they had much in common. They both capitalised on traditional material as the root source of musical learning, and each went back to first principles in formulating a developmental learning sequence (see Taylor, 1979). Murphy concluded his article by summing up the convictions he thought the two men had in common as far as music education was concerned: music should be taking place all the time in schools; there should be a music lesson every day; wherever possible the teacher should be a specialist.

There were mixed messages in all this. The Orff developments were associated with costly instruments, and a move towards music teacher specialism, and hence towards curriculum isolation. This sat uneasily with the training college tradition of MEUT concerned with dealing effectively with the musical training of classroom, generalist teachers. To an extent the Orff movement trickled down inappropriately from secondary schools, which were having to cope with severe criticism about music being regarded as the most boring and useless subject in the curriculum (Schools Council, 1968). Orff's practical method seemed a lifeline.

Much creative work in secondary schools also related to a close identification with the musical avant-garde. In line with the expansion of MEUT to cater for the under thirteen's there were several demonstrations of creative work from secondary schools, culminating in a demonstration from Tom Gamble and his pupils from Manland School (MEUT *Bulletin*, January 1978). They worked on a piece called 'Dust of Saturn' and the commentator in the Bulletin detected influences from Berio. It was reckoned to be a fascinating glimpse into what true 'creative' work could be.

But a significant comment came from committee member, Anna Mendoza, herself a noted music educator:

> if only we had his (Gamble's) knowledge and understanding of modern music, and if only we could release the shackles of our own conventional musical education enough to extend our musical boundaries without discarding the music of the past. (Ibid., 5)

By significant I mean this avant-garde approach of Gamble's demonstration unintentionally exhibited a degree of musical knowledge and understanding of contemporary music that was inhibiting to the primary school music teacher.

To sum up, the ideas of creative music making were promulgated by the Association, in tandem with a commitment to child-centred education. But progress in this direction appeared to be diverted by imported methodologies, an emphasis upon teacher specialisation, and by a style-centred approach to musical creativity stemming from the secondary schools.

It would be misleading to suggest however that the Association pursued progressive ideas in a monolithic way. There is much evidence in the archival sources about concerns to preserve and modify traditional approaches to the teaching of music, particularly singing and musical literacy.

4. Traditional Concerns

At the very first conference it became apparent that the technical and the aesthetic needed to be held in balance. Elizabeth Barnard agreed that movement might help children understand the relation between high and low pitch. But she found a neglect of pitch and melody in the teaching of infants. There was still a place for the teaching of traditional songs as a vehicle for tonic sol-fa and hand signs, but it should be developed in tandem with creative work through question and answer responses (MEUT *Bulletin*, October 1949). This was echoed by Anna Mendoza in considering 9-11 year olds. She hoped that there might be progression, increasing the range and complexity of intervals through singing. Why not introduce Purcell, Schubert and Brahms as a change from the ubiquitous folk songs? But the dilemma for her, was how to make the dreary process of reading music enthralling. Certainly sight reading should not be divorced from real music. But she also believed that the encouragement of creating original tunes and rhythms should make children aware of the need to have a permanent record, realising that only through learning the ABC of music 'can they capture and keep their own music, and get a glimpse of the vast world of music around them when the teacher is not there to act as a medium' (ibid., 20).

These two concerns about the teaching of singing and musical literacy sustained the attention of the Association throughout its life. There was a problem with the common practice of massed singing, whereby two or more classes gathered together under the direction of the music teacher. An editorial in the *Bulletin* (June 1954) called for the disbanding of formal singing, because education should be thought of in terms of experience, experiment and activity in constantly changing groups. The classroom should become a music workshop.

John Horton attempted to develop singing in new ways (MEUT *Bulletin*,

July 1959). He regretted that singing tended to become formal and stylised in school communities. To illustrate his point about the informality of traditional music making he introduced a recording of an Indian weaver singing at his work, with an accompaniment based upon the intricate system of rhythmic counterpoint dictated by the loom. We have only to look at young children at play to observe such spontaneity. Horton asked how could the class teacher introduce children to the art of music without losing this sense of spontaneity. Mass organisation tended to dampen such enjoyment. He regretted that many teachers had large massed choral classes foisted upon them. After all, he stated, we are teaching music, not striving for choral effect.

Four years later Gerald Trodd (HMI) (MEUT *Bulletin*, February 1963) was finding that too frequently he found large numbers of children standing in serried ranks for a lesson, singing national songs or hymns, often chosen unwisely. For many children, singing at school might be the first experience of hearing old tunes. One small boy had immediately recognised 'Bobby Shaftoe' as the 'Esso' tune! This experience emphasised for Trodd, the importance of maintaining our teaching of traditional tunes and rhymes.

One way of revitalising singing was the adoption of the Kodály method from Hungary. Cecilia Vajda, a Kodály advocate and disciple expounded the method at the March 1968 conference (MEUT *Bulletin*, July 1968). In an editorial it was admitted that singing had become the Cinderella of music in the classroom. Too frequently pitched percussion and unpitched percussion instruments took pride of place:

It is quite unfashionable nowadays just to sing for the sheer pleasure of singing. Always something else must be going on at the same time - movement or instrumental work. (Ibid., 1)

However the editor had reservations about adapting a Hungarian method to English schools: 'one would find it difficult and perhaps not necessarily desirable to apply the same rigid disciplining of procedure in our classrooms'.

Hand in hand with concerns about singing were worries about the level of musical literacy. To Gerald Trodd it was clear that at junior school, children should be required to read from notation. It safeguarded the heritage:

Until the skill of reading music is mastered, the children are an easy prey to the commercial music just round the corner. (MEUT *Bulletin*, February 1963, 5)

Kenneth Simpson from the Central College of the London University Institute of Education asked whether it was possible to teach reading to ordinary children in the ordinary class (MEUT *Bulletin*, February 1966). He reminded his audience of the era of payment by results, whereby sixpence was granted if the children sang by ear, and one shilling was the allowance if they could read music. Simpson believed teaching music reading was important if it was remembered that reading was not an end in itself. If the spirit of music is lost in a mechanical process of reading it is worse than useless. He considered that teachers had to set children thinking by means of symbols. The ear must first be trained by experience, and then by reading, which in turn will then help aural training. Simpson advocated the use of letter names to give absolute pitch, and tonic sol-fa to demonstrate function.

Nine years later a special session was organised entitled 'Ways to Musical Literacy' (MEUT *Bulletin*, February 1975) which attracted a large attendance. Geoffrey Winters outlined different kinds of notation, and admitted that much music required little notation, but without a knowledge of it, music was difficult to learn and explore. Cassette recorders could be useful in encouraging children to think of different methods of notation. However, Winters was convinced that if children were to get the most from European traditions then we must teach notation in schools. But, the sound must come first. Finally in discussion, Kathleen Blocksidge felt that the reason for the decline in the teaching of musical literacy lay in the cutting down of time given to music in Colleges of Education, especially in helping students to be prepared to teach music in Primary Schools. The issue continued to concern the Association. New and reformed ways of teaching it were outlined by Candida Tobin and her Colour Music System (MEUT *Bulletin*, February 1977), and Bernarr Rainbow with his exposition of the New Curwen Method (MEUT *Bulletin*, January 1981).

In this discussion about traditional techniques I have focused upon singing and musical literacy. What arises is the evident desire of the diverse members of MEUT to integrate these concerns with the more experimental ideas concerning musical creativity.

5. Conclusion

MEUT represented a link with pre-war music education, based on percussion bands, pipe making and playing, movement, and orchestral work. Essential to its existence was the need to develop a greater unity within music education. Certainly, many of these influences coalesced and formed fresh alliances.

In its early years MEUT associated with progressive educationists and attempted to bring music education into a relationship with contemporary ideas. The outcomes were its debates and demonstrations on creative music making. In making explicit the often implicit assumptions that lay behind the original intentions of the founding musical groups and in relation to the broader-based educational associations, such work gained in strength. Of course creative music making was not new. We have already highlighted Walford Davies's attempts to engage children in tune-building which had been at the forefront of the BBC's school music broadcasts since 1926. But what was different and characterised the MEUT's discussions was their child-centredness. The Association had also to cope with cross currents, notably with the powerful Orff and Kodály lobbies, and the style-centred avant-garde secondary school creative music movement. There were also genuine attempts to reconcile the traditional activities of singing and musical literacy with these new ideas. MEUT represented the liberalism of the training colleges and colleges of education, with its attempt to integrate the essentially pre-war notion of massed musical activities into the new freer environment of primary schools.

But during the 1970s the very existence of the system of teacher education and training was 'deliberately destroyed' (Dent, 1977, 156). The proposals for colleges of education merging with other colleges or polytechnics to become major institutions of higher education contained within it the threat of closure for many of the colleges that were deemed to be too small for such an arrangement. This combined with a steep drop in the birth-rate which greatly lessened the demand for teachers, and the severe economic recession culminated in three rounds of cuts by 1980 which resulted in closure of many colleges and departments (Gordon, Aldrich and Dean, 1991). With these amalgamations and closures, MEUT's power base was virtually destroyed. In-service work with teachers tended to pass into the hands of the local education authorities. Also, with the publication of the Black Papers (Cox and Dyson, 1971), MEUT had become out of step with the times. It was too fragile to be able to confront different perspectives, symbolised by an editorial written by Blocksidge in 1976 (MEUT *Bulletin*, September 1976, 1):

> The theory that primary education should be based on what children like to do is being seriously questioned, not only by parents, but by teachers and educationists alike. Is the correct balance being maintained? Are essential skills being omitted?

But the real achievement of MEUT lay in its persistence in attempting to break the mould of restrictive thinking about the music education of young children, and the placing of experience rather than information at the centre of the process.

In my analysis of the contribution of MEUT to primary school music I have attempted to deal with curriculum as a historical process. I have examined ways in which a subject association helped to define and defend a subject (see also Jenkins and Swinnerton, 1996; Knight, 1996). It is admittedly difficult to be certain what impact MEUT had on the everyday practice of its members. Furthermore there is a suspicion, that in transmission, innovative curriculum ideas can become parodies of themselves. But, nevertheless, research into such associations enables us to investigate the genesis and evolution of new ideas and opportunities within the curriculum, as well as the persistence and resistance of traditional methods.

This tension between the innovative and traditional paradigms of music teaching is highlighted in the next chapter's account of the two Schools Council's music projects for primary and secondary schools in the 1970s.

5 'A House Divided': Music Education during the Schools Council Era of the 1970s

The image of the curriculum as the site of a battleground over values and beliefs (Kliebard, 1995) is helpful in a consideration of music education in the United Kingdom in the 1970s which was strikingly characterised by Swanwick as 'a house divided' (Swanwick, 1977). The division was between a model of music education which was subject centred, and one which was child centred. Musically, according to Swanwick, the former represented skills, literacy and the value of the Western music tradition, whilst the latter encompassed experiment, creativity and an emphasis upon contemporary developments in music (ibid., 67).

The purpose of this chapter is to investigate the impact of the work of the Schools Council's Music Committee on music education during the 1970s, with particular reference to its two curriculum development projects in music that came to symbolise the polarity which Swanwick described. In order to place the discussion in a wider frame, I shall also consider the stance taken by the Music Committee about the relationship between music and the other arts-based subjects in the curriculum. I shall ask the following questions: what was the context in which the Music Committee carried out its work? What factors influenced the development of the two projects? What were their similarities and differences? What were some of the causes of their apparent polarisation? What wider impact did the work of the Music Committee have on the furtherance of closer links between music and the other arts?

1. The Schools Council and its Music Projects

The Schools Council for the Curriculum and Examinations was established in 1964, a child of that optimistic and buoyant decade. Financed jointly by the Department of Education and local authorities it became the major curriculum development body in England and Wales until its demise in 1984 (Plaskow, 1985). The Schools Council came to represent the ideology of teacher control and autonomy in relation to the curriculum, and crystallised the devolving of curriculum and teaching to the teachers (Simon, 1991). It is worth bearing in mind, however, that most of the Council's projects came to fruition in the 1970s, which was a stormy decade in the UK with the oil price crisis, the series of bitter miners' strikes, and the ensuing radical cuts in public expenditure which particularly affected education (ibid.). Peter Gordon (1989) has helpfully characterised the history of the Council as follows: An Age of Expansion (1964-1972); The Difficult Years: Growing Centralism (1972-1977); Reappraisal, Reconstruction and the end of the Schools Council (1977-1982). This chronology should help us in finding our bearings.

In 1967 a Music Committee was set up under the chairmanship of Myers Foggin, Principal of Trinity College of Music, London. Succeeding chairmen were Allen Percival, Principal of the Guildhall School of Music and Drama (1968-1972), and Jack Dobbs, Vice-Principal, Dartington College of Arts (1972-1978). Its members comprised teacher representatives from primary, secondary and higher education, in addition to Schools Council staff and an HMI (in the role of assessor). The remit of the committee was: to keep the music curriculum under review with reference to courses, teaching methods and examinations in schools, to identify matters which appeared to merit investigation, and to initiate proposals for research development and associated in-service training (25 January 1967, Schools Council (1967) Music Committee (hereinafter Music Committee), PRO EJ2/38). Subsequently three sub-committees were set up dealing with Advanced level work, primary and secondary schooling (March 1967, Schools Council (1967-1978) Music Committee, PRO EJ1/156).

At its second meeting on 1 March the chairman considered the implications of the influential Plowden Report, *Children and Their Primary Schools* (CACE, 1967) which, as we have seen in previous chapters, had castigated music teaching for its reliance on mass instruction, over-direction by the teacher and a lack of any notion of individual progression. The attention of the Music Committee was drawn particularly to the lack of continuity and follow-up between primary and secondary schools. Members were informed that it was not uncommon for a child to leave primary school with a high standard of music, only to enter a secondary school whose music was only a nominal activity. Music teachers in the different sectors, it appeared, were ignorant of each other's worlds. The Committee identified the ending of this irrational situation as one of its urgent priorities. Other aspects of the discussion arising from Plowden included the crucial position of the non-specialist classroom teacher, musical literacy and the adverse effect of pupils' inability to read music (1 March 1967, Music Committee). At a subsequent meeting (23 June 1967) the Primary Sub-Committee reported that according to the DES only four per cent of teachers had undertaken a specialist academic course in music, and were thus qualified to teach the subject. The Sub-Committee members recommended more in-service and curriculum courses with less academic emphases, to ease the severe situation.

It was in the context of the severe criticisms contained in Plowden, that Arnold Bentley from the University of Reading, was asked to address the Music Committee on past and current research in music education (25 October 1968). Bentley believed the aim of scientific research in the field should be a better understanding of children's development through an education in music. He felt such research could be directed towards the production of a core curriculum which could be taught by a non-specialist teacher. Bentley advocated some form of common musical achievement test, combining aspects of those of Wing, Seashore and himself. Significantly there was a question from a committee member, which prefigured future controversy, as to whether there might be a clash between such research and the accepted principles of education for children under seven, based upon discovery and exploration. Bentley replied that there was no such conflict.

By June the following year (1969) a research proposal submitted by Bentley had been accepted. It was called 'Music Education of Young Children'. There were three aims: to increase understanding of how children learn in music; to clarify and define the aims of music education for nursery and primary school children; to produce guides and materials to help teachers achieve these aims. The project was initially funded for a five-year period with a grant of £38,500 (Schools Council, 1972a).

Before tackling the Music Committee's secondary schools remit it is necessary to provide some contextual background. One of the Schools Council's early policies in the wake of the Newsom Report *Half Our Future* (CACE, 1963) was to prepare programmes for the raising of the school leaving age from 15 to 16. As part of its preparation, the Council commissioned from the Government Social Survey a large-scale enquiry into the attitudes of parents, teachers, pupils and ex-pupils. This unique report, *Enquiry One* (Schools Council, 1968), was a damning indictment of music: it was judged to be irrelevant in the school experiences of young school leavers. To emphasise the bleakness of the findings, the report went on to contrast this apathy and indifference with the vibrancy of young people's musical culture outside of school. As a result of the report's overall critique, the Schools Council identified as one of the most pressing needs, a reappraisal of what was offered to the young school leaver under the heading of humanities, including music.

Early consideration within the Secondary Sub-Committee encompassed the needs of both the unmusical or anti-musical child, and the talented pupil. It was thought that an investigation of the two extremes might lead eventually to the musical needs of the average child (23 June 1967, Music Committee). Other priorities were seen at this early stage as providing guidance to teachers about the desirable balance between creative and theoretical studies (ibid.), and a consideration of music's contribution to the extra year of schooling that pupils would be taking when the school leaving age was raised to 16 (17 November 1967, Music Committee).

There was no doubt in the Sub-Committee's mind that considering the place of music in secondary schools was to open a veritable Pandora's Box (23 February 1968, Music Committee). But HMI Ronald Roberts, a member of the Music Committee, pointed out that the main task of the group was curriculum development. Changes in organisation might have to be confronted if effective music teaching was to take place. We might note at this point that Roberts was a key figure behind the scenes of the project. Paynter observed that as staff inspector, Roberts was anxious to find an answer to the anomaly that although young people loved music outside school, inside school they positively hated it (see Griffiths, 1977).

The Music Committee's first report, *Music and the Young School Leaver: Problems and Opportunities* (1971) attempted to press the claims of music in the curriculum. Its publication arose out of some discussion on the part of the secondary sub-committee about the implications of *Enquiry One* (25 October 1968, Music Committee). It was agreed that this had reflected many inadequacies in the teaching of the subject, but should not be taken 'as indicating a total failure in the teaching of the subject'. A suggestion had been made that a paper might be drafted on the child who rejects music. Caution was advised as it might prove discouraging to younger teachers.

At a later meeting of the Music Committee (27 January 1970), the chairman of the Working Party responsible for the report, Jack Dobbs, pointed out that a disturbingly large proportion of music students were reluctant to enter the teaching profession under the present conditions of working. Worryingly, if they happened to become teachers they sometimes chose to teach subjects other than music. What was needed was to set out the cause of dissatisfaction with the conditions of teaching music in schools, in the hope that the authorities would be induced to improve them: *Music and the Young School Leaver* was the result.

A key observation of the published report was that if real progress was to be made towards making music an integral part of the educational process for the secondary school pupil, experimentation could no longer be left entirely to the individual teacher. New ways of working would only be possible within the context of the whole school: for example the extended day might be introduced, with the result that so-called extra-curricular activities would become an equal partner with the rest of the educational programme. But there should also be possibilities of music teachers getting together on an area basis to develop curriculum ideas.

Its recommendations and conclusions make interesting reading. It was recognised that some young people tended to reject formal education in the arts, although experience showed this was not necessarily final. But schools in turn could no longer disregard the emergence of a teenage sub-culture. Moreover, a creative or an experimental approach to class or group music making was often found effective with older pupils: there was no doubt that training in notation should be practical, and not restricted to traditional forms. Interdisciplinary work, temporary integration of departments were all to be welcomed. Such developments might allow older pupils to follow music courses on an optional basis.

The report pointed to the work of the North-West Regional Curriculum Development Project (NWRCDP) as an exemplar of teachers becoming practically involved in experimental work. This project (supported by the Schools Council) had its own music panel which met between 1967 and 1970. Its membership reflected its collaborative nature, with representatives from a university, a college of education, LEAs and teachers. The project's work was based in the relatively new Teachers Centres in the north-west. The panel's report was published as *Creative Music and the Young School Leaver* (NWRCDP, 1974) and described work in classrooms which utilised simple instruments, based upon a growing interest in the creative aspects of music making. Music teaching objectives were developed under the headings of creative, re-creative and listening activities.

It is characteristic of the project that its report focused upon teachers developing ideas in the classroom. Three chapters are devoted to the work of three separate teachers who in turn emphasised music making, musical insights and co-ordination skills. In its conclusion the report points out that the teachers saw in creative music activities a possible means of maintaining an interest in the subject. The team's task was not merely to suggest opportunities for personal expression 'but also to recommend means for making that expression purposeful and insightful' (ibid., 79). The report has received little critical comment and yet in many ways it fits into the action research case study model. It was a significant precursor of what was to become the Schools Council's Secondary Music Project.

On 12 October 1971 John Paynter from the University of York, whose influential book, *Sound and Silence* (Paynter and Aston, 1970) had been recently published, addressed the Music Committee to put forward ideas for a proposed project 'Music in the Secondary School Curriculum'. The proposals concerned the role that music could play in the total process of education at secondary level. The purpose was to change attitudes towards the subject (*Music in the Secondary School Curriculum News Sheet* [hereinafter *News Sheet*], Spring 1974). Paynter advocated practical aspects of both creating and performing music, but wished to avoid putting forward 'creativity' as a panacea for the problems of music in schools. In his view making a division between creative and performing aspects was artificial. The Music Committee agreed Paynter had put a good case, and the project was to commence in Autumn 1973 (12 October 1973). It was funded initially for £40,000 for a five-year period (25 April 1972, Music Committee).

2. Music Education of Young Children 1970-1976

The primary music project team comprised Arnold Bentley as director, and two researchers as deputy director and project officer. Bentley envisaged they would be aided by experienced teachers.

There was no doubt in Bentley's mind that the optimum time for music as a part of general education was in the early years of childhood. Until improvements had been more widely achieved at this level 'compulsory music lessons for older age groups is often a waste of time' (Bentley, n.d.).

As one of its first tasks, the team carried out a survey of music in English primary schools (Schools Council, 1973) with information gathered from 200 school classes and from 150 other schools. The findings reinforced those of Plowden. There were five main impressions: widely differing approaches, conditions and standards of achievement concerning music teaching in this phase; a lack of aims, or of any general agreement about them; the need for teachers to receive simple guidance in the teaching of basic musical skills and understanding; the low priority afforded music reading; the differences in attitude between boys and girls with respect to music lessons even before the age of eleven.

But the survey was most revealing in the lengthy commentary on the policy and organisation, contents and methods of music education. It was noted that Plowden had looked in vain for an awareness of individual progress in music, and could find little evidence of assessment. The project might well develop Music Achievement Tests which could provide a means of measuring individual progress within a class. But above all what primary teachers wanted was a clear structure:

> It seemed to the majority that the more important goals of music education, particularly practical and reading skills, could be achieved only through a carefully 'structured' course in which regular, short spells of teaching and practice bought the best result. (Ibid., 162)

There is no doubt where the authors' interests lay: teaching music reading was a priority. The benefits were clear: there was a limit to what could be learned by rote or played by ear; musical notation was helpful as a visual aid to listening; the difficulties of learning notation were frequently exaggerated; children needed to work in an environment where notation was continually used. Finally, teachers might borrow some helpful techniques from the field of the teaching of verbal reading.

The problem according to the team, was that such teaching was seen to be unfashionable. Children were now able to use avant-garde techniques in the classroom and produce compositions instantaneously. But what was required was a balance. At a meeting of the Consultative Committee we learn of the considerable reservations the team felt about the term 'creativity'. It was imprecise and led to misunderstandings. Moreover it had even acquired moral overtones. Instead the team felt that 'originality' would be preferable (11 March 1971, Schools Council (1971-1978) Music Education of Young Children Consultative Committee, University of Reading (hereinafter MEYCCC)).

Finally the authors of the survey re-stated their conviction that the traditional methods of playing, singing and literacy provided scope for truly educational purposes. But they warned against complacency. Music education was placed in a vicious circle: teachers' weaknesses were blamed on colleges who in turn blamed secondary schools, who depended upon the primary schools. It was the project's task to enter this circle.

Alongside the survey the deputy director, Rupert Thackray, worked with teachers on small-scale projects (Thackray, 1974). His doctoral study, supervised by Bentley, had focused upon the measurement of rhythmic abilities (Thackray, 1969). It is not surprising therefore that testing was the key to these projects: it was used to find out more about children's abilities in different musical areas, and to assess a particular teaching method or form of presentation. Amongst the testing-related topics were a Music Achievement Test, a test of the understanding of musical concepts, and a test relating to a tape recorded lesson.

Congruent with this was a scheme, developed by the team, for what they termed 'Basic Music' which was to be derived from a core curriculum. Underpinning it was a conviction that children are stimulated by a sequence which provided a consistent, logical and comprehensible 'map' of music (Schools Council, n.d.).

1973 was a crisis year for the project: both deputy director and project officer left to take up academic posts elsewhere. Strong feelings about the project had been expressed by members of its Consultative Committee. In particular there were 'varied views' on the value of printed guides and on testing (25 January 1973, MEYCCC), and the possible misuse of achievement tests by teachers (30 January 1973, Music Committee).

In a letter from Bentley to Ian Parry of the Schools Council (19 November 1973, Schools Council Correspondence) it was reported that one member of the Consultative Committee thought that the project should be closed 'and the Schools Council cut its losses'. Bentley was upset that no other members of the Committee had refuted that outright condemnation. He spoke directly:

> This strong criticism, coupled with doubts about the future puts the project, and my part in it, into an area of uncertainty, and for me personal concern ... on a project which apparently merits so little approval.

The chair of the Consultative Committee, Allen Percival, resigned and Jack Dobbs took his place on 30 October 1974. However, the project weathered the storm, and two new members of the team were appointed. Thackray's successor as deputy director was Iain Kendell whose doctoral research, supervised by Bentley, was to focus upon the teaching of basic musical literacy (Kendell, 1979). On taking up his new position Kendell explored various avenues of change open to the project (Kendell, 1984). It had been made clear to him in top-level discussions that, in the context of the national economic downturn triggered by the oil crisis, there was no intention to provide adequate funding to effect educational change via in-service training. Moreover, as has been mentioned in the previous chapter, teacher training was appearing increasingly fragile, with the wholesale mergers and closures of colleges taking place due to restructuring, and the decline in the birthrate which meant a decline in the number of teacher training places that would be required (Dent, 1977). Kendell became convinced that in these straitened circumstances faith would have to be placed in the publication of new classroom materials to effect change.

Kendell's article, 'If you can teach reading you can teach music' (Kendell, 1976) encapsulated his belief that classroom teachers were as capable of teaching the basics of musical literacy as they were of teaching reading. But music appeared to lack completely the concept building materials so familiar in the teaching of language and mathematics (Kendell, 1974). This led him to believe that if suitable materials were developed, most primary teachers would be able to teach music literacy effectively.

It is worth elaborating on Kendell's thinking at this point. His doctoral dissertation (Kendell, 1979) investigated the learning processes which led to the attainment of music literacy. Although this was the focus, he was keen to point out that the ideal Primary Music Curriculum was a balance between the development of the child as The Listener, The Creator, The Performer, The Literate Musician.

But it was with The Literate Musician, defined as someone who could both read and write music symbols with understanding, that Kendell was preoccupied. He wanted to devise a complete scheme for teaching musical literacy. But whereas in his literature review he found that there were indications that it was possible for most young children to learn to read music, there was no research to suggest practically how this could be achieved. In the published schemes of work he surveyed, he found little agreement beyond presenting rhythm notation ahead of pitch, introducing the crotchet, minim and two quavers first though not necessarily in that order, and deferring the teaching of 6/8 time until after the introduction of the dotted crotchet and quaver. All of the schemes, Kendell believed, assumed a degree of music knowledge greater than that possessed by many primary school teachers.

In his experimental work, Kendell closely monitored 24 children of different general abilities on a weekly basis for two years. They worked with the project's trial materials which covered eight areas of learning: Visual Discrimination and Visual Recall of Music Symbols; Concept Formation; Acquisition of Musical Vocabulary; Physical Co-ordination Skills; Auditory Disrimination and Musical Memory; Music Reading; Musical Writing; Creative Skills (ibid., 122). After a pre-test which established a 'base-line of musical illiteracy', the children he observed worked with identical materials in pairs, operating cassette tape recorders and/or responding to printed work cards. Of the 24 case-study children, 16 became fluent music readers and the remaining eight made significant progress. Kendell (ibid., chapter 6) claimed that a number of new factors with regard to how children learn in music had been revealed. He highlighted six of these:

- poor pitch singers were helped to sing in tune by use of tape-recorded material and by the kinaesthetic aid of playing glockenspiels/xylophones;
- fluency in reading and performing rhythms was gained by all the case-study subjects;
- it was not necessarily the best music readers (or singers) who achieved the best auditory discriminations in rhythm and pitch;
- essential factors for all children to become fluent music readers included: practice in the visual discrimination of music symbols; a highly structured programme; practice in copying music and in grouping notes; mental rehearsal of the task;
- a widely based programme was necessary, including listening, singing, playing, creative work and concept-building stories, games and activities;
- with the need for constant reinforcement of knowledge and the highly individual rates of progress of the children it was clear that a class music lesson once a week was not a situation in which children could be reasonably expected to learn a basic music literacy.

Kendell's work on the Schools Council primary music project gathered pace. He and his team developed a structured programme for the beginning stages of music education, suitable for use by the non-specialist teacher. The project materials were developed as kits which focused on the teaching of music through story, introducing basic musical concepts and skills reinforced through games of all kinds. Alongside language master cards which gave practice in notational skills, there were 'creative cards' which encouraged children to improvise. Although the basic literacy skills were seen as a means to an end, it was emphasised that creative or re-creative work could not be achieved without them. It became essentially a musical literacy scheme (Kendell, 1977)

Faith was gradually restored in the project. But at the Music Committee meeting (4 June 1974) there were still reservations which the members wanted to record. Some disliked the use of the term 'musically illiterate teachers' in the project materials, whilst others were concerned that the kits might come to be seen as a syllabus which might consequently stifle creativity and imagination.

Between 1976 and 1978 the project's materials were published as five substantial boxes or kits of materials, intended to cover the entire primary school age-range (Nursery Stage, Infant Stage, Link Stage, Junior 1 Stage, Junior 2 Stage). It was called *Time for Music* (Kendell, Allin and Walkley, 1976/78). The critical reaction was mixed. J. David Boyle (1979), a respected American music educator, admired the scope of the publication, but had a real concern about the utilisation of music reading as something of a challenge and end in itself, rather than a means for extending and broadening musical experience.

The review by the musicologist Robin Maconie in the highly influential *Times Educational Supplement* (1 April 1977) was savage. Maconie had no time for programmed music teaching, because it held that children acquired musical skills in discrete and measurable stages, and could therefore be taught music in a series of matching stages. But worse, this 'whole dreadful concoction (was) to be administered by untrained personnel'. Far from teaching music to children, the project promulgated a system of teaching in order to furnish teachers who did not know any better with a rigid code of practice.

This understandably provoked heart-searching within the Schools Council. Jasmine Denyer, one of the Council's officials on the Music Committee gave her response to a colleague (18 April 1977, Jasmine Denyer to Mrs White, Schools Council Correspondence). She maintained that the primary project did very well what it set out to do:

> I would defend its objectives in the same way as I would defend the teacher of mathematics who insists on children learning their number bonds and learning their tables.

As a postscript, Brian Fawcett (1982) underlined the fundamentally problematic nature of the project in an evaluation he conducted in some Gloucestershire primary schools. He found the responses to the singing tests he administered to children undertaking *Time for Music* worrying. Half of the children sang the exercises as monotones. Fawcett wondered if this was the result of the project's strategy of encouraging children to de-code through the medium of the glockenspiel, as it was perfectly possible to sightplay without actually listening. It was the lack of the development of the inner ear that was problematic in all of this. The project's materials

> do enable children to make a start in the de-coding process via a glockenspiel but the same glockenspiel may very well be a barrier to real understanding. (Ibid., 14)

In retrospect, Bentley felt the project was out of step with the prevailing educational mood, although he believed it had made an impact on the teachers and schools for which it was designed (Bentley interview, June 1998).

3. Music in the Secondary School Curriculum 1973-1980

John Paynter's initial course team comprised himself as director, together with an assistant director, and a research officer. It was Paynter's conviction that it was not enough to look at better ways of teaching established music techniques. Music was an important factor in that part of the curriculum that dealt with the emotional needs of young people. Essentially the project was 'an educational experiment and not a purely musical one'. This was a once-in-a-lifetime opportunity, to extend on a national level work that had been going on at the University of York, at the same time emphasising that 'educational reform starts in the classroom' (*News Sheet*, Spring 1974).

There is no doubt that the mainspring of the project lay in Paynter's own experience as a composer who became a school teacher. The ideas he began to develop in the 1950s about musical education and classroom techniques became the basis of his subsequent thinking about music in schools. It was largely Paynter's own classroom music teaching and the strategies he evolved, that informed his views about the possible directions for the project. However, we should also note the wider context, and in a number of key articles Paynter has alluded to some of the historical and philosophical underpinnings of the project. He situated it within two traditions: the creative/inventive/interpretative aspects of music that from the 1950s had been the driving force of such teacher composers as George Self, Brian Dennis, and R. Murray Schafer; the encouragement of children's expressive responses to the arts in schools rooted in the highly significant work of Herbert Read in art and David Holbrook in English (*News Sheet*, January 1979). The title of Read's book *Education Through Art* (1943) was significant for Paynter. The problem in music education had been that understanding music had become synonymous with knowing about music. But Read's point was that we only come to appreciate Art through our own creative efforts. For Paynter the principal objective of teaching music was to encourage musical understanding, an appreciation from the inside.

He attacked head-on the vexed question of musical literacy in an article entitled 'Don't let them drive you dotty' (*News Sheet*, June 1976). Humorously he observed that 'a severe attack of spots before the eyes has been known in some classrooms to prevent people from hearing any musical sounds at all' (ibid., 9). He was adamant that 'you can't teach music like reading'. There was no comparison, music is not like words. Paynter admitted that sadly the dilemma in school music teaching concerned the place of notation. Here we see a direct conflict with the ideas of the primary project: it exposes a fundamental faultline running through music education between the technical and the aesthetic.

Paynter contrasted those who saw music as a 'cultural' recreative art which addressed a small audience, with his own aim to embrace all pupils through 'the education of the feelings and the development of sensitivity, imagination and inventiveness' (ibid., 10). This desire for inclusiveness prompted him (*News Sheet*, April 1978) to plead that the arts should develop joint representation in order to counter their neglect on the curriculum. There was no need to be defensive. The arts after all were important educationally because they presented us with the possibility of organising our experience:

> Artistic enterprise is indeed a way of 'saying' something personal, but it is also a means by which we may discover ourselves and crystallise that discovery in what is made - a piece of music, a painting, a poem or a dance. (Ibid., 12)

The project was unashamedly teacher centred:

> we believe that educational reform starts in the classroom. We are, therefore, looking to teachers to propose further research topics. (*News Sheet*, Spring 1974, 1)

A distinction was made between pilot schools and trial schools. The former were expected to guide the project in developing patterns of experimental work, whilst the latter were invited to evaluate these materials by classroom use.

When it came to the project devising and utilising materials, however, there were two problems to be faced. First, it was becoming apparent that there was a preponderance of work with the younger age group in the secondary school (3rd meeting, n.d., 1975, Schools Council (1974-1980) Music in the Secondary School Curriculum Consultative Committee, hereinafter MSSCCC, PRO EJ1/51). Jasmine Denyer later suggested that the project team should be devising materials, particularly where there was a gap, for example with the 14-15 year olds (7 April 1976, MSSCCC). Providing for the needs of this age group was clearly problematic and lay behind a question from the Consultative Committee: were conventional classroom instruments suitable for teenagers? The reply by the team is characteristic of its principled and perhaps rather high minded attitude:

> the material of music is sound, not instruments, and it was at the crucial age of 13 that children begin to feel the self as the centre of experience - thus we shall be seeking to stimulate working processes which start from the individual rather than from materials and instruments. (3rd meeting, n.d., 1975, MSSCCC)

With this mention of adolescents, it is worth making a detour to discuss the considerable thinking by those associated with the project, about the place of pop music in the classroom. Piers Spencer (1974), in a working paper, argued that as pop was central to the lives of adolescents it made sense to use it in the classroom, and he described work with a group of children in which they were asked to write blues or music for a radio commercial. He used pop to enable pupils to 'express something more personal, more sincere' (ibid., 5). One of the problems he found was that traditional classroom instruments were considered old-fashioned by the pupils. But Spencer was not a lone voice.

In a speculative paper for the project, on how children think musically, Robert Bunting (1976) outlined a possible way forward by referring to the main modes of musical perception, and how we might evaluate individual progress through understanding the stages at which children might encounter these. For example, he maintained in the primary and lower secondary stages that children might show an equal interest in the following modes of composing: Illustrative (giving music meaning by association e.g. 'thunder', 'anger'); Vernacular (working within the language of our familiar everyday music e.g. pop songs, TV themes, jingles) and Speculative (developing musical ideas). However, Bunting believed strongly that the later stages at secondary school witnessed a narrowing down of these modes to the Vernacular: it was essential therefore that teachers engaged with the musical tastes and experiences of adolescent young people.

One of the refreshing attributes of the secondary music project was its diversity of outlook (at least within its own ranks). It clearly enjoyed controversy. Sally Daunt (1976), for example, found that pop music was not necessarily the key. She felt it encouraged passive listening, invoked rivalries between different camps, and was generally (since the Beatles) of a low musical standard. She found her grammar school pupils wanted to be musically literate, and to know about the Elizabethan period, or the life of Schubert.

To get back to the main argument, however, the second problem being encountered by the project was that teachers were experiencing difficulties. On the one hand the inexperienced appeared to grasp new materials as ends in themselves, whilst on the other hand the more experienced were finding it difficult to truly sustain creative work over a long period. The development of a sense of progression was regarded as a vital concern (3rd meeting, n.d., 1975, MSSCCC). The ideas were sometimes found threatening or unattractive by teachers:

> I must be going wrong. Our children are not enthralled by experimenting with sound. They dismiss it as 'kid's stuff' ... Classes of 32 uninterested children do not want to play games, but to take part in 'real' tunes and 'real' songs. They are happier singing traditional rounds rather than 'messing about' as they put it. (*News Sheet*, January 1975, 10)

Roy Cooper, the project's deputy director, acknowledged the problems (*News Sheet*, June 1977). Many teachers had joined the profession to perform music, but now they had come to realise that the real needs of the classroom were different. This could lead to confusion and bitterness, as there had to be a coming to terms with a new set of aims, in the process overcoming fear of the unfamiliar.

The project was keen to be mutually supportive of music teachers in bettering their working conditions and the status of the subject, through tackling accommodation and timetabling. Improvement in the design of music rooms and suites in schools was a priority. In the final report of the project, Paynter (1982) addressed the results of his consultation on the subject with HMI, architects and the DES, under the heading 'Making Room for Music'. He was less successful in his desire to experiment with the fundamental reorganisation of the timetable, that in many ways was a key to implementing a more enlightened policy towards music in schools (3rd meeting, n.d., 1975, MSSCCC). Schools might temporarily suspend the timetable for an arts project, but there was little interest in radical permanent change.

By the end of its life the project had devised a series of tape-slide programmes (later published in video format with additional commentary recorded to camera by Paynter) which provided a platform for teachers to explain their own beliefs about musical education in schools, and to give examples of how they were attempting to work out those beliefs in practice. The programmes were intended to provide food for thought, and give some indication of current classroom practice in various parts of the country. They included work with the integrated arts, creative music workshops, music in inner urban schools, and the compositions of pupils and their relationships with the work of other composers. The project also produced two films: *Arrangements,* which described interpretative work at Trinity School, Warwick, and *A Place for Music* which showed classroom work from five schools, in which various approaches were adopted to encourage creativity.

The project was not short of critics. Hancox (1988) questions the role of Roy Cooper as deputy director. Cooper possessed a clear and uncompromising vision of music education, which was frequently seen as hostile, revolutionary and anarchic by some music teachers and local authority advisers with its emphasis upon the contemporary and the avant-garde.

Some of the project's presentations unnecessarily polarised opinion. For example Keith Swanwick (1975) gives an account of a workshop given by Alan Vincent, the Schools Liaison Officer. The gist of Vincent's message was that asserting that schools should impart knowledge and skills was 'naive and insensitive'. In 'creative music-making' there was more emphasis upon group awareness, sensitivity and sheer fun: imagination comes first, skills follow after. Its purpose was to allow children to find their own true selves.

Swanwick had a problem with 'creative music-making': 'is there such a thing as non-creative music making?' (ibid., 9). And worryingly he wondered about the relation of the practical activities to the project's philosophy:

Out came Roy Cooper's flash-cards of different colours and shapes to which one has to make a response in sound. These were followed by the improvisation of vocal counterpoints whilst crawling across the floor, a game called 'Hello' where people call out their names in the rests of a rhythm pattern, and finally a performance of *My Bonny Lies Over the Ocean* during which we had to stand up or sit down on every word beginning with the letter 'B'. All good fun but hardly conducive to an individual's imaginary journey. (Ibid.)

Of course with hindsight we can now view such an event as a rather apt manifestation of the style of the *zeitgeist* of the 1970s.

Hancox (1988) itemises other problems. The aims of the project were not sufficiently well-known outside of its own circle (although admittedly the circle was not that small, consisting of more than 200 schools in England and Wales). The materials tended to have an amateurish feel, produced as they were by teachers without the aid of consultants. Finally the whole structure of pilot and trial schools was considered by Hancox to be unwieldy.

In his valedictory personal view of the project, Paynter (*News Sheet*, January 1979) restated his conviction that there must be a long term effect from such a project. He wondered if the right questions had been addressed, however. At the start of the project, Paynter reflected, there was an urgent need to do something about music in the curriculum, but he asked, was there really a widespread feeling that the answer lay in articulating a clearly argued educational background? Perhaps music teachers had been more concerned that a national project might simply raise the status of music in schools. Paynter identified an intractable problem:

It would seem that for many teachers music is still an exclusive rather than an inclusive area of the school's work, and it is now quite fashionable again to argue against the idea of 'music for the majority'. Sights are often firmly set only on the able musicians who can be trained. By comparison, the broader educational values of the subject seem to be tame and irrelevant. (Ibid., 2)

It had been Paynter's belief that the only 'rule' in music was the ear, and that essentially music was an aural experience. Critics had identified the project with 'self-expression', but they misunderstood. It had been tarred with the brush of using 'modern methods' which allowed pupils to wander aimlessly without any kind of guidance in a world of self-discovery, unhindered by traditional values. But what the project really offered was a chance for pupils to undertake work which involved creative and interpretative decisions. This was applicable across the whole ability range since it relied fundamentally on a sensitivity to sound: 'it is sounds we must work with, not information about sounds' (ibid., 3). It was this process, in Paynter's eyes, that offered something of educational value: it involved real opportunities for the interpretation of information and for decision taking.

The problem was twofold. First, it was easier and quicker to feed pupils with information and formulae. Second, music was allocated so little time in schools. Consequently the achievements for many would be humble, and could be dispiriting. Fundamentally, however, Paynter maintained that the project had demonstrated that it was still possible to involve pupils in exciting and productive musical work of a creative nature.

There were dilemmas which concerned the evaluation of the project and the assessment of children's creative work, both of which emphasised the distance between it and its sister project. The matter was raised at an early meeting of the Consultative Committee (28 September 1974, MSCCCC). If the central aim of the secondary project was to change attitudes towards music, in what ways could it be evaluated? Suggestions were made about diaries, questionnaires and case studies. Paynter was somewhat dismissive, because he wanted a clear focus. He elaborated at the next meeting (3rd meeting, n.d., 1975, MSSCCC). Evaluation of a tangible statistical kind was an impossibility, since the project was concerned not with any finished products but with the exchange of ideas. The appointment of an external evaluator would detract substantially from the main work of the project. Anyway, he argued, the people who should carry out the evaluation were the children themselves, or a spearhead group of teachers in the area organisations.

This suspicion of formal research procedures and their relation to music making (which he was later to change his mind about), was mirrored in a later statement by Paynter regarding the obligatory assessment of pupils' practical musical work by teachers: 'it seems to me such a silly thing to want to do' (Salaman, 1988, 31). But in an earlier more considered way Paynter had clarified his ambivalence (1977). He believed that activities which involved the use of pupils' imaginations and inventiveness were notoriously hard to evaluate. It was not possible to measure artistic ability and its effect without selling the subject short. Perhaps the most that could be achieved was to observe some development of a pupil's expressive ability and control of the medium.

Swanwick (1975) was critical of the lack of evaluation of the project's musical activities: to say evaluation was impossible was evasive, especially when it was argued that there were real developments between first and third year pupils in their creative music making. He made a plea for the systematic collection of impressions.

In retrospect, the dependency of the project upon composing in small groups might be seen to have been its Achilles Heel. We have already noted the difficulties teachers were experiencing in such work in Chapter 3. A measure of detailed assessments and evaluations of pupils' work might have presented a warning light. Bunting's working paper (1976) pointed out the danger in his rather uncomfortable yet prophetic message to those involved in a project which had fundamentally explored classroom composition through group activity: group music making was not the way forward, 'we must aim for a position where individual work is a normal occurrence' (ibid., 10). Warming to his theme, Bunting exclaimed that individual progress had to be demonstrated, and individual scope could not be provided with a regular diet of group work. He recognised the pragmatic reasons for the present emphasis, but warned 'if we continue in this way we may end up cutting our own throats' (ibid.).

In spite of the energy and momentum of the project, Paynter's last report 'in the field' to the Consultative Committee was muted in tone. He was disappointed that the objectives had so often been misunderstood, and questioned whether the present climate was any longer right for such innovative work (22/3 April 1978, MSSCCC).

3.1 Music and the Integrated Arts

Running alongside the development of the secondary project was a continuing discussion in the Music Committee about the role of music *vis-à-vis* the rest of the arts. We have previously read of Paynter's desire to break down the barriers. But the extent to which subject barriers should be relaxed was a dilemma, because the benefits of working together might be outweighed by the possible disappearance of music as a discrete subject from the curriculum.

One of the Schools Council's preoccupations was with General Studies for the 14-16 year old age group. It was spoken about in terms that favoured subject integration. At a meeting of the Music Committee (13 October 1970) the view was taken that integration was not necessarily a sound philosophy whether or not it was dressed up as 'creative arts', 'expressive arts', or simply 'the arts'. The arts may be a generic grouping, but they each worked in very different ways. A working party was set up to consider the matter. This group next reported to the Music Committee on 26 January 1971. It was having problems: on the one hand it was difficult to find out information about actual practice in schools, and there was controversy about distinctions between 'combination' and integration'. Two years later its report was produced, *Music and Integrated Studies in the Secondary School* (Schools Council, 1972b).

The first chapter surveyed music in the integrated primary school curriculum. The greatest emphasis was upon the links between creative music making and environmental studies. There are descriptions of music in classrooms describing a gathering storm, using bonfire night as a stimulus for some rhythmic speech and percussion work, and music making after a visit to a local river.

In secondary schools the theme of the environment was again a key to such work. In an outer London girls' school, pupils were encouraged to make landscape music: a townscape, a pastoral scene, a jungle scene, a mountainous landscape, and a waterfall. But there were other outcomes of integration utilising music and art, and music and poetry. The 'grouped arts' were allocated two half-days a week in the lower school. In another school in the same area, integration of the arts and humanities had taken place for classes in the first three years, so that music as a separate subject was not timetabled. The effect of integrated studies upon the pupils had been 'amazing'.

In all of the work observed the main tension had been the balance between the subject and the project. But occasionally this was achieved. For one teacher the main value of such work was that children came to discover parallel concepts in the arts, like rhythm, tension, relaxation, space and form.

The second part of the report focused upon conclusions. There was a difference between correlation, combination and integration. In the first two of these approaches each subject remained virtually intact within the traditions of its own discipline. True integration, it was suggested, could only take place at the creative level. If music's prime educational function was to symbolise emotional experience, and if its strongest claim to be an educative medium was its creative character, it followed that music could only find common ground with other disciplines if they contained a creative element. But the report stepped back somewhat from the implications of all this, and admitted that in practice too hard and fast a distinction between combination and integration should not be insisted upon. Nevertheless, there was a danger that music may be weakened further by ill-considered projects:

Any attempt to invoke the principle of integration as a pretext for reducing time-allowances for the Expressive Arts should be vigorously resisted. (Ibid., 27)

A further problem concerned the musical child, who frequently found little of stimulus in such work. Again, there was a fear that music in combined projects had little hope of independent survival.

Finally, the report pointed to the social benefits for pupils and teachers through the experience of working in teams: it might help motivate the majority of pupils 'aware of no particular gifts or enthusiasm for music' (ibid., 30). Nevertheless under no circumstances should the purpose-designed musical groups, such as instrumental classes, orchestras, bands and choirs, be allowed to disband in favour of this newer approach.

In a contribution to the debate, Bunting (1976, 16) expressed his position eloquently

Music certainly needs to be revitalised by contact with the other arts; but it must also be revitalised from within by a new approach to its basic elements ... Rightly handled, this polarity between the arts as separate disciplines and the arts as an expressive unity could be a rich source of creative teaching and learning.

The ambivalence of music educators regarding integration and combination is further illustrated in the reactions of the Music Committee to another of the

Schools Council's projects, 'The Arts and the Adolescent' (see Schools Council, 1975). The Committee invited the project's directors, Malcolm Ross and Robert Witkin, both from the University of Exeter, to a meeting, as it had been asked to recommend approval for a one-year follow-up with a possible two year extension to the project (27 April 1971, Music Committee).

Witkin explained that the project had commenced with a discussion concerning the functions of the arts in general education, and then had worked towards specialist areas. The intention was to develop curriculum materials, but first there needed to be a firm conceptual basis. It had been found that music as a curriculum subject had had difficulty in maintaining its position in pupil esteem, in maintaining the morale of music teachers, in technical resources, and in developing appropriate modes of evaluation. If music could be placed in a clearer educational perspective, the problems of teaching it would be seen to be comparable to those of 'the arts'. An extensive research programme had been undertaken in 36 schools to explore the basis of children's preferences for various musical activities, to evaluate types of lessons witnessed, to interview teachers, and to classify the large sample of children in respect of their attitudes towards the arts. The variables that effected music in schools were enumerated: fourth-year pupils had the most negative attitudes towards the subject, sex differences played a part, but social differences were not significant.

The Music Committee's members were not impressed. While the project might have proved its value as an exercise in social science 'it was questionable whether musicians had been sufficiently consulted on specialist matters'. Serious doubts were expressed about the basis of the questionnaire that formed part of the public survey. The project might appear to have gone beyond its original brief.

At its next meeting (12 October 1971) the Committee expressed a lack of confidence in the Interim Report, both in its form and content. Findings were derived from the questionnaire which was not included, there was also no evidence that the expertise of music specialists had been drawn upon. It simply covered much of the ground of the committee's working paper on *Music and the Young School Leaver*, and added little that was useful.

Malcolm Ross emphasised that one of the aims of the project was to help teachers create their own programmes and materials by giving them a conceptual basis for their subject. Part of the project's brief had been to establish a basic model which would allow for

tracing a pattern of emotional development and superimposing on that a plan for the development of the arts in education. It was believed that a parallel existed between emotional and intellectual development and that there was a tendency in adolescence to synthesize experiences. Once a common language for the arts had been found in terms of emotional experience a way would be open for the exploration of the problems of the separate disciplines with the aid of a small group of expert consultants.

We may note here some similarities with Paynter's convictions about the power of the arts as a curriculum force. But the Committee remained sceptical and suspicious that the project was hostile to music. For example the project had pointed out that only a small number of music teachers had attended refresher courses, but there was no comparative data concerning teachers representing the other arts. The interim report gave rise to serious concerns about form and content, and clearly the project directors had not established a clear understanding with specialist musicians. The Music Committee's decision was unambiguous:

> As far as it effects music ... the committee must record its dissatisfaction with the proposals, and would have no confidence in the continuation of the enquiry on the lines set out in the proposals and in the Interim Report.

It saw a danger that such a report 'might lead to negative conclusions which could have a discouraging and depressing effect on work in the schools'.

In the following year (10 October 1972), the Music Committee again was faced with a proposal from the project. Again members expressed their frustrations. It was all very well pointing to the shortcomings in arts teaching which were familiar, but no solutions were proposed. Although it was agreed to earmark funds for a new project, the Committee had no great confidence in the proposer being able to carry out the project effectively as far as its musical context was concerned.

The Music Committee was next asked to approve the proposed publication of the project's book, *The Intelligence of Feeling*, authored by Witkin (1974) (3 March 1973, Music Committee). It was felt many teachers would have difficulty in understanding it, and that the text might have been relieved with rather more concrete examples. Moreover, the references to art works in schools appeared rather extreme. Nonetheless it was agreed that the work presented a very original and significant thesis, which could have considerable effect.

The last contact with 'The Arts and the Adolescent' Project by the Music Committee concerned a report prepared by Ross (2 October 1973, Music Committee). Again the mood appears to have been hostile: there were a lot of unnecessary materials, and there were misreadings of several publications on music education. Paynter intimated that he took exception to some of the comments on current developments in music education. The Committee agreed that the report should not be published as a working paper, but rather as an abstract in pamphlet form.

What lay behind this unease with the questions of integration and closer collaboration? There is clearly a sense of defensiveness which permeates the discussion. First, there appeared to be little substantial evidence of effective work across the arts in schools. Second, there was the shared concern that music was the most vulnerable partner in these activities. Third, Ross and Witkin appear to have touched a raw nerve about music's problems, which had the effect of uniting opposing musical factions into an isolationist position.

4. Discussion

It will be apparent that the divisions that surfaced within music education, and between it and arts education were profound and deep-seated. The Schools Council's Music Committee had indeed opened up a Pandora's Box. For Jasmine Denyer from the Schools Council, the division within music centred upon two schools of thought, one that children's music should comprise children creating their own music, and the other more concerned with children re-creating other people's music. Because the latter purpose had been so ingrained, Denyer argued, the advocates of creative music had had to overstate their case, and neither side would attempt to bridge the gap. In hindsight she felt it unfortunate that the two projects had appeared to reinforce this division (18 April 1977, Schools Council Correspondence).

Jack Dobbs was rather more optimistic about the division in a report he produced for the Music Committee in 1977:

> Although the two projects are separate entities, with their own philosophies and ways of working, it is important for the Committee to look at music education as a whole and to identify elements and approaches which are common to both projects and which make for continuity throughout school life ... During the last fifteen years the scope of music education has increased so considerably that many teachers are bewildered by the number of approaches and varied types of activities available to them. Nevertheless, there are encouraging signs that the current re-thinking and re-assessment going on throughout the country are beginning to sort out the wheat from the chaff, and the essential from the peripheral. (7 September 2000, quoted in letter from Jack Dobbs to Gordon Cox, in Cox Correspondence)

What comparisons can be made between the two polarised projects? First, they both connected with significant government reports which cast serious doubt upon the effectiveness of music education in primary and secondary schools. Consequently there was a crisis which had to be addressed.

Second, both projects were based in universities, but from within two very different traditions. The project based with Bentley at Reading, 'Music Education of Young Children', was located in a Department of Education, and Bentley's own work had focused upon the development of musical aptitude testing in the tradition of Wing and Seashore. Consequently, Bentley was interested in developing a project as a piece of 'scientific research'. Testing was an important ingredient in the early stages of the project, and the development of a structured sequential music curriculum able to be taught by non-specialists became the eventual aim. The project directed by Paynter at York, 'Music in the Secondary School Curriculum', was placed within a Department of Music, established in 1964, known for its innovative and wide-ranging courses, with a particular focus on composition. In an interview, Paynter exclaimed 'primarily I am a composer, not an educationist' (Salaman, 1988). Perhaps his emphasis explains why the division between the two projects was profound, representing the distance between the 'educator' and the 'musician', symbolised in the contrasting institutional cultures within which each project was based. Central to Paynter's purpose was the promotion of informed discussion on the role of music in the curriculum. His resistance to formal evaluation was symptomatic of his desire to concentrate on ideas rather than products. With such opposing ideological views it is hardly surprising that there was little agreement between the two projects concerning for example musical literacy or musical creativity. The positions were entrenched. What complicates the picture, however, is the impact 'The Arts and the Adolescent' had in uniting the Music Committee in opposition to a project that had much in common with the secondary music project. It seemed that music was prepared to strengthen its own place on the curriculum, but was defensive and hostile to other members of the arts community.

Third, the two projects emphasised the role of their teachers differently. At Reading the project was undertaken by trained researchers, aided by experienced teachers working within a structure of trial and associate schools. It was research led in a top-down fashion. The York project, however, was teacher-centred: it was the teachers in the pilot schools who initiated materials and ideas. The distinction appears to have developed due to a difference in the perception of research, on the one hand as something highly specialised and technical, and on the other a process in which teachers can participate on an equal footing as researchers in order to improve their own practice.

Fourthly, there was a difference of scope. The York project attempted to extend the boundaries of music teaching, to embrace the arts, and to develop new ways of timetabling, and of designing music rooms. It wanted to effect a change in teacher thinking. It dealt with difficult and demanding areas of fundamental change, and thought of its work as radical and extremely challenging (31 January 1978, MSSCCC). In contrast the Reading project focused upon a less global aim, to develop an effective way for classroom teachers to teach music literacy in primary schools. It did not require the fundamental change of classroom teaching method which the York project demanded.

Finally, the directors of both projects questioned whether their work was appropriate for the stormy and eventually bleak educational and political contexts of the 1970s.

5. Conclusion

What can we learn from this story? Kliebard (1995) has likened the different platforms for restructuring the curriculum as part and parcel of a national morality play. There is little doubt who the hero has been in this musical play. Undoubtedly the York project has played a profound part in shaping contemporary music education. Its most substantial contribution was to establish classroom group composition (for good or ill) as the basis of the music curriculum. It undoubtedly influenced (aided by the work of Swanwick, 1979), the General Certificate of Secondary Education (GCSE) in music with its practical hands-on approach. Patrick Salisbury, Staff Inspector for Music (HMI), told Hancox (1988, 231):

> The GCSE criteria really are there as a major representation of the Project ... These criteria could never have been as they are without the Project.

The influence continues in the National Curriculum with its emphasis upon composition and musical invention.

But quite apart from allocating winners and losers, a consideration of the work of the Schools Council Music Committee may help us in illuminating some of the fundamental beliefs about music education that were being contested in the 1970s, and their connections with structures and institutions. The following related oppositions have been apparent: primary/secondary schools; university departments of education/university departments of music; top down 'expert' research/practitioner research; focused limited change/wide scale and structural change; musical literacy/creativity; materials/processes; testing/expressive response; basic music/education of the feelings; music/the arts. I am not suggesting a simplistic correspondence here, but an understanding of these apparent dichotomies and an investigation of their complex interlinking may enable us not only to better understand why music education in the UK in the 1970s was a house divided, but more crucially to learn some lessons for the future.

6 Talking about Music Teaching: Recollections and Realities

In her groundbreaking book *Governing the Young* (1989) Barbara Finkelstein outlined succinctly the tendencies of educational historians to emphasise 'the normative rather than the actual, prescription rather than practice, the 'ought' rather than the 'is' in classroom procedure' (ibid., 36). Consequently there is a 'silent history' concerning the typical activities of teachers and pupils in schools.

The intention of this chapter is to uncover something of this 'silent history' of music teaching, by listening to the recollections and stories of both experienced secondary school music teachers, and of student music teachers. Too often the voices of such practitioners are ignored and dismissed as being simply anecdotal. What I wanted to do was to document their experiences in their own terms of living music in schools.

To achieve this intention I tape recorded interviews with 20 secondary school teachers and student music teachers, all of whom worked as mentors or trainees within the Reading University/Schools Partnership, which prepares students on the one-year Post-Graduate Certificate in Education (PGCE) course to become music teachers in secondary schools. Individual interviews were conducted between 1995 and 1997 (Music Education History Archive, University of Reading). In format the interviews were semi-structured with freedom for my informants to develop their own themes if they wished. After the interviews were fully transcribed I analysed the data, searching for categories and ideas. Subjective understandings of experience are central to this chapter, and indeed provide its structure. Consequently I have incorporated my informants' ideas in their own words as much as possible, derived from transcribed portions of the tape-recorded interviews.

The chapter is in two parts. The first considers ten student teachers' recollections of their own musical education, their eventual decision to train to be music teachers, and their early experiences of teaching. The second considers the realities of the work of ten experienced music teachers in schools. It is hoped that such a group biography will provide a detailed picture of the processes of becoming and being a music teacher.

1. Student Music Teachers Talking

Before outlining the details of the interviewing procedures that I carried out for this study, I shall briefly summarise some of the main developments within music education that had occurred since the early 1970s which was when the majority of my informants were born, bearing in mind the point that subjective perceptions are incomplete without historical context (see Goodson and Walker, 1988).

The seventies, as we have seen in the previous chapter, were the years of intensive curriculum development within music teaching, coming to terms with the severe criticisms of traditional music teaching, outlined in the Plowden (1967) and Newsom (1963) reports.

By the time most of my informants were in secondary school the Department of Education had published its guidelines, *Music 5-16* (DES, 1985). This looked forward to a cohesive and coherent music curriculum throughout a child's life at school, based upon practical music making. By 1988 the first General Certificate of Secondary Education (GCSE) examinations had taken place, with the radical emphasis upon composing and performing. Seven of my informants took this examination, indeed one was in the first cohort.

Towards the end of the majority of the students' lives as school pupils, the Education Reform Act was passed (1988), which was to lead to the introduction of the National Curriculum (1992). The Act marked a watershed in education in general, and teacher education in particular. Judge *et al* (1994) have isolated three examples of this profound change: centralisation of control by government; a technicist vision of teaching by government whereby teacher education reverts to teacher training; opening teacher education to market forces. Also considerably affected was the structure of the provision of instrumental teaching in schools, which by and large became privatised. By the time the students arrived for their PGCE year in the mid-nineties, the university course had been undergoing a radical shake-up, with the government insisting on more school experience for students, greater collaboration with schools, and teachers being involved in admissions, assessment and supervision (DES circular 24/89 (DES, 1989), and DfE circular 9/92 (DfE, 1992)).

The first interviews were conducted with each of the ten student teachers near the beginning of their PGCE course. There was a follow-up interview after the major teaching block. Of the ten students, six were female and four were male; seven were between 21 and 22 years old on entry to the course, and three were in their late twenties or early thirties; eight had read music at university, one had read civil engineering, and one had attended a music conservatoire; one student had gained a Master's degree; all of the students were new to Reading University.

In my interviews I focused on:

- to what extent student teachers were musically socialised within their families;
- how they perceived their own music teachers and their own musical education at school;
- why they decided to read music at university, and then to train to become a secondary school music teacher;
- how they characterised their early experiences of teaching.

These four perspectives provide the framework for the ensuing discussion of student music teachers' experiences of formal and informal music education.

1.1 Music in the Family

In his review of the literature on the use of biography in understanding teacher behaviour, Knowles (1992) identified remembered childhood experiences of learning, and of family activities and family role models, as major components of teacher role identity. Woods (1984) underscored the influence that early life experiences had on the present elements of a teacher's life and work. In her study of four student music teachers, Schmidt (1998) paid particular attention to family experiences, and noted that when her informants confronted classroom management problems they frequently drew on their negative memories of themselves as children in families.

Families can provide their children an opportunity for musical socialisation. Certainly, the family, and particularly parental interest, is often the crucial factor influencing *which* children participate in musical activities at school (see Finnegan, 1989). To what extent were the student teachers I interviewed, socialised musically within their families? None of the parents were professional musicians or music teachers, but they displayed an impressive list of musical interests. Nevertheless, my informants would generally preface their observations somewhat apologetically by saying 'my parents aren't really musical, but...'

There were two students whose parents' musical development matched their own. In one case the mother's interest coincided with that of her son:

> as my interests grew and I became more and more passionate about music, so did she ... we fed off each other almost, you know, interests and passion.

Eventually she started to sing semi-professionally on the club circuit, 'standard easy listening, Whitney Houston, Shirley Bassey ... the sort of stuff that goes down well in the kind of clubs she used to sing in'. Another student's father developed a similar reciprocal relationship: 'since I've started doing music, he's now actually taken up singing'.

Most parents were interested in listening to music. One father was particularly influential on his son:

> My dad is a great fan of late nineteenth-century classical music ... when I was a kid he was really into Russians ... Borodin, Tchaikovsky, Bizet (sic), Rimsky-Korsakov ... the only thing he actually said I should listen to was Rite of Spring ... I was absolutely appalled by it, and it scared me witless.

More typical however were parental preferences for popular music ranging from experimental sixties music like Frank Zappa, to Acker Bilk and Frank Sinatra. One student remembered the significance of her own reaction to a popular music TV show, which prompted her family to seek musical tuition for her:

> It all started off watching Top of the Pops ... I was at my nans ... and I was listening to 'In the Jungle' ... and I was dancing away as you do, and then I went over to the piano and picked out the tune ... so they found out I could do it ... so she (nan) paid for the first piano lessons.

Most of the students I interviewed received a similar level of positive musical encouragement from their families. These reminiscences are typical:

> There was a couple of guys who lived in the close near us who played in brass bands, and I could hear them practising, so I started asking my dad if I could play, so he took me round ... my grandma bought my first trombone ... my mum saw an advert in the paper ... they were starting a sort of jazz swing orchestra up;

> I can remember coming home from school with songs that we'd sung at school, and playing or singing them to my mum, and she'd say 'Oh, I remember that'.

From the often apologetic tone in which they talked of their musical backgrounds, it became apparent that the students appeared to recognise only performing abilities as the criteria as to whether their family was musical or not. Listening preferences appeared to be discounted, particularly if, as in the majority of cases, they related to popular traditions. Definitions of what constituted being musical seemed to narrow as the students became specialists themselves.

Perhaps by uncovering and developing respect for their own early musical socialisation within the family, students might be helped to recollect memories of themselves before they became 'musicians', so that they could relate more empathetically to the parallel experiences of their pupils, in addition to questioning their own assumptions about what counts as music.

1.2 Remembrances of Music in School

In his discussion of the formation of teacher role identity, Knowles (1992) identifies the crucial influences on future teachers of their memories of average and mediocre classroom experiences, and of positive teacher role models. Likewise, Huberman (1993) emphasises that former teachers, particularly those held in high esteem, strongly influence those who wish to become teachers themselves. Frequently they are chosen as personal and professional role models. Schmidt (1998) found that her four student music teachers appeared to derive the majority of their teaching practice from their own experience as pupils.

My informants' own views of their music teachers can be seen to fall into the three categories of positive, ambivalent and negative perceptions. The most positive recollections related to their teachers' youthfulness, friendliness, openness and liveliness. One of the students explicitly drew a parallel between the professional qualities she wanted to develop, and those of her own secondary school music teacher:

> I sort of didn't take part at all in music till about the third year, and the music teacher said 'get your act together and do something' ... (she was) quite young and friendly really, very nice, sort of made you want to get involved, and I think I'd like to be in a position as a teacher to offer that to somebody else.

These same characteristics were associated in the following testimony with a young 'very bubbly and lively' music teacher who demonstrated a revelatory way of teaching through an informal style which emphasised individual musical creativity:

> She was quite free with ideas ... she was quite happy to let you go out of the class ... she'd quite happily let you go and play in the hall, or we used to play in the changing rooms at one point, and she'd have people all over the place and it never seemed to worry her ... she was very into composition, she wanted everybody just to go off and write pieces in groups.

All this exercised a profound influence on my informant who became fully engaged in composition at school:

> I frantically wrote songs ... love songs, typical teenage girl ... I'd write them in harmony ... it was me and three boys who were all doing GCSE music, all ended up setting up this band which was awful (laughter) ... but it was good ... because we wrote things as a band ... you could record them pretty simply ... we played in assemblies ... it went down well, yes, and we had our own T-shirts and all, and we thought we were it ... Hot Ice! (laughter).

The student was to follow this passion at university.

The ideal music teacher combined liveliness and friendliness with an evident desire to communicate a love of the subject. For example one popular teacher was a jazz sax player, who was 'very lively, very bouncy, a big sort of chubby man ... a very fun person and was so enthusiastic about everything'. His influence was such that 'the music in the school was definitely him'. But there was even more to this teacher. He was meticulous in his organisation, and fair in his allocation of scarce instrumental resources to pupils, so that eventually everyone would have a chance at some point to play keyboards or drums.

The notion of meticulousness can be extended to the ability to communicate musical knowledge clearly and memorably. This picture of a piano teacher nicely encapsulates the combination of patience and clarity:

> She was really good, she was not that brilliant herself, but she was very patient with me ... I needed someone gentle who just explained things to me ... I remember when we did dotted rhythm ... I remember having tears about that, so she cut an apple up and showed me. I just ended up eating it.

Another student's much-regarded teacher had been a professional trumpeter who had had to relinquish for personal circumstances a brilliant big band career. He became an instrumental teacher and combined care for his students, with informal and highly effective teaching:

> so he ran, he needed a bit of cash, so he ran this composition course, charged a fiver for it ... I said 'look I can't pay a fiver, I haven't got money like that, my mum and dad certainly haven't.' He said 'look, don't say anything to anybody, but you'll not pay'. So I used to go to this thing on a Saturday morning ... and he'd show us how to arrange bits and bobs of like sort of Blue Moon ... and he worked on this basis, sort of chords work ... it's amazing, six-week harmony lesson ... it was like a really laid back way of doing it.

The emphasis upon youthful, lively, committed music teachers was not the whole story however. Eccentricity held its own fascination, as in this recollection by a student, of her sixth form teacher:

> he was one of those wild old Brahms figures, and he was absolutely batty ... but he was the most amazing, so inspirational, so enthusiastic ... this great big beard and hair ... he did not distance himself, if he was having a bad day he let you all know.

For this student the music teachers who stuck in her mind were those who demonstrably loved the subject: 'they could tell me the grass was blue'.

As a footnote to student teachers' positive experiences of music at school, there is no doubt that extra-curricular activities including bands, choirs and orchestras were highly valued. Frequently these groups met away from the school, and gave concerts in prestigious venues. This was also the case for those who found their musical salvation in community music making ensembles. In his discussion of Austrian music education, Mark (1999) makes the point that such groupings motivate pupils towards a common goal, and therefore raise the prestige of music in schools. The experience is best represented by these comments:

> I absolutely loved playing in orchestras ... and that was a big turn-on because I got into the County Youth Orchestra when I was about 15 ... I suddenly realised how wonderful it was ... it was quite a hierarchical system;

> I used to stay all Wednesday night for about four hours going to all these orchestras ... you could work your way up: you started off the lowest of the low, you would be leader of your section, and then you would go up an orchestra.

Sometimes, however, the richness outside the instititutional gates of schooling was sampled, particularly with choral groups, brass and swing bands. It could lead to television, radio and theatre work. The process in brass and swing bands was not so hierarchical as the county orchestral schemes, but through it we sense this informant's progress:

> (between 15 and 18) I was playing at the Albert Hall ... doing television ... meeting a lot of musicians, listening to jazz funk ... it really sort of opened me up to music ... we were playing on a small scale at professional level.

It was this sense of professionalism that shines out of such experiences as another student reminisces about his brass band days:

> we had these little books with a list of gigs that we were doing, and there were loads of them ... I was getting absolutely fanatical about it ... it lasted for about ... three years, it died a death.

Some students were ambivalent about their school music teachers. This was caused by being scared of certain teachers, who nevertheless achieved impressive musical results within their schools. Underpinning this ambivalence was the perception that music was for the favoured few (of whom these students were included). One of the problems that emerged in my informants' recollections, was the difficulty teachers faced in treating musically experienced and inexperienced children together, sometimes in spite of the best intentions:

> I remember ... everyone playing instruments in the class, and people who could play an instrument ... we'd sort of get in the centre and play ... those instruments and everyone else ... would play glockenspiels, or percussion ... and we'd do class things like 'Eye Level' ... I mean I thought they were good, but they did sound a bit ... they sounded very glockenspielly, and I think the people who didn't learn instruments felt a bit out of it, they felt they were the thick ones.

The ambivalence some students harboured about their music teachers was frequently caused by the distinctions these teachers made between their musical sheep (the able musicians) and goats (the rest). Several students reported that they found it socially difficult to be identified as a 'musical sheep' in comparison with their 'musical goat' peers.

The development of a more practical curriculum at GCSE sometimes effected change for the better. One teacher was recollected as 'a bit of a Hitler', with little interest in the majority of pupils who she deemed to be unmusical. Her teaching methods were formal and unmotivating. But, interestingly, a slight change for the better occurred with the introduction of the GCSE syllabus:

> She almost became slightly more approachable ... she was giving us more freedom, more choice, she was giving us lots of ideas composition wise ... The listening side of it she still maintained her old style.

Negative memories of music in school included some bad experiences at primary school, which resonate with the folklore of being taught music:

> I was told I wasn't musical ... by one of my music teachers ... because she said I couldn't sing in tune and she didn't like me being in the choir ... I was put off music ... and I found it embarrassing and quite humiliating most of the time.

Others recollected rebelling against the musical inexperience of their primary teachers and the dragooned teaching of massed singing.

At secondary school, some teaching styles were felt to be inappropriate. For example, one music teacher was over-extrovert in his approach, and singled out individuals embarrassingly:

> He'd make us come in and stand round in a horseshoe and sing things on our own, and at thirteen you don't want to do that anyway.

Other negative impressions were caused by disorganisation and subsequent lack of control and inappropriate or unstimulating ideas:

when they were doing things like composing ... looking at stuff to do with wind going through trees and all that, it just seemed to me totally meaningless ... everybody else in the group treated it as just an hour to mess around in;

We were always writing about *Danse Macabre* ... and it meant nothing to anybody. I mean it's like 'think about spooky things and draw a picture of what this is about' ... the music lessons were absolutely appalling, more *Danse Macabre*, more copying out of text ... I mean no-one liked music.

The reasons for such negative remembrances of music teachers and their teaching were various, and might be seen as the reverse of the youthfulness, openness, friendliness, liveliness and musical communication we noted in connection with influential teachers.

In considering these reminiscences there is ample scope for clarifying what makes for quality music teaching. In his study of an exemplary music educator, King (1998) isolates four attributes of music teacher effectiveness: high level verbal and non-verbal language; routines and organisation which provide the framework for artistry in teaching; humour; the creation of a quality environment. We have noted some of these issues in relation to the meticulousness of organisation, and effective musical communication of some of my informants' teachers, as well as the reverse.

1.3 Deciding to Become a Musician and Music Teacher

In his study of the lives of teachers, Huberman (1993) reports on the 'hesitations' individuals have between choosing what different subjects to specialise in, and between various careers. For example: does an individual choose a subject to study because of its intrinsic interest, or because it will land a job? Is a career chosen because it is potentially fulfilling, or because it has high status?

The decisions of my informants to study music at university or conservatoire were not taken lightly. There were other options, indeed one student entered university to read politics, but changed after eight weeks, 'I just missed it (music) too much ... I just thought, what am I doing?' Others had to decide between music, English, maths, and art. However, music usually won out because of the strength of its attraction: it was natural, 'my heart was really in music'. One student remembered being told by a careers teacher 'do the thing you enjoy, because at the end of the day, even if you don't achieve as much, you'll enjoy it more, and ultimately it will work out that you'll become better at it'. Perhaps the decision to take music was best summed up in one student's testimony as follows 'there was always something about music which just completely drew me in'.

Whilst at university most of my informants found their thoughts turning towards teaching. When we consider their motivations for teaching it is helpful to bear in mind Huberman's (1993) discussion on the subject. The classic motives, he suggests are 'contact with young people' and 'desire to share one's knowledge'. These he calls active motivations. But there are other varieties. For example, material motivations for teaching include becoming financially independent, having favourable working conditions, whilst passive motivations involve a choice of teaching 'for lack of something better', or through simply 'sinking into it'. When we consider music teachers' motivations we need to take note of what Mark (1999) calls the music teacher's dilemma: musician or teacher? This partly relates to status. In his study of the Vienna Hochschule, Mark noted 'a prestige problem' that separated musicians and pedagogues, to the latter's disadvantage.

We might divide my informants' decisions to enter teaching into the straightforward and committed, and the provisional. But frequently the motives were mixed. One student was committed to teaching from the age of 14. The subject kept changing, but the goal did not. What was crucial was her love of being creative, whether in writing stories or in composing music. The only reason she applied for university was that eventually she would teach (although she veered away from this a couple of times). Practical reasons entered into it as well:

> I was thinking ... by that time I was engaged, so I wanted at some point to be able to settle down ... I wanted to have some money, and then the reality of it all came into play, and you know, there was something about the security of teaching that appeals to me a lot.

A strong motivation is successful experience of prior teaching (see Knowles, 1992: 131-2). For music students this is often deeply significant, because of the manifold opportunities to teach music privately:

> That became clear really in the sixth form when I had some private piano and clarinet pupils, I just found it easy to put across the ideas ... I do love teaching music ... I love inspiring other children.

In a related way, a mature student working in a very different context of professional jazz funk playing, found in his leadership a model for teaching:

> At the same time I was running my own bands ... and that in a way is like being a teacher, you control the situation.

Others had less straightforward motivations. For example one student had wanted to be a teacher when she was at primary school, but at secondary school she became hostile to teachers and consequently changed her mind.

Eventually teaching became just one of a series of options. The most common alternative to teaching amongst my informants, was further study of music at post-graduate level. Funding was a major problem however, and so teaching was selected as a second-choice. One student asked rhetorically of teaching as a career, 'how many teachers can say it was their first choice?'

At least two of the students chose to teach because the professional musical life placed personal demands on them they could not meet, so teaching became an alternative:

I felt very nervous and my memory kept going;

I have not got that arrogant drive that most performers have ... people have often said ... 'Oh, you'll make such a good teacher'.

Much of this discussion resonates with the findings of a questionnaire survey of the views on school music teaching as a career of over 400 second-year music students from universities and conservatoires (Poulsen and Macleod, 1999). It was carried out partly to understand more clearly the reasons for the current serious shortfall in recruitment in the UK of student music teachers who wish to teach in secondary schools (see Coll, 1998). The 'idealism' of those with positive attitudes is contrasted with the 'worldliness' of those with more negative perceptions. Positive views of music teaching included: love of children and subject; a belief in the power of music to provide enjoyment and communication with others; a conviction in music's inherent worth as a curriculum subject. Negative attitudes were associated with: poor career prospects; unattractive working environments; personal reasons mostly concerned with working with children and the desire to enter the music profession; perceptions of the low job satisfaction of teaching music (see also Mark, 1999, for similar findings).

1.4 Experience of Teaching Music

When student teachers actually start to undertake practical teaching on their courses, their teacher role identity is put to the test. Bullough *et al* (1991) discuss this experience in terms of a process progressing through fantasy, survival and mastery. The boundaries of these processes are necessarily blurred and overlapping. Nonetheless these stages provide some context for my informants' overview of their student teaching experience.

By the beginning of the main school teaching block of ten weeks half-way through the course, eight of the ten students remained (two had left before the teaching practice commenced, deciding that a teaching career was not for them). By the end of the block teaching only one of the remaining eight students had experienced real problems. He came to realise that these stemmed from his difficulty in relating to pupils: 'I simply didn't relate, didn't show interest in them ... I wasn't deeply fond of most of my pupils'. He felt it was a characteristic problem of musicians like himself who had trained to be soloists: it was deeply rooted in his personality. This opinion resonates with Bouij's (1999) study of music teacher role identity in which it was observed that many who class themselves as Performer, fail to distinguish that a Pupil-centred role exists.

Two other male students were reflective about shortcomings in the nature of the music curriculum in schools, as a result of their experience. The first became dissatisfied with the way he taught composing in the classroom without any kind of context. He had a passion for history and desperately wanted to tell his pupils about the background of the music they encountered. There needed to be more to music in schools than being able to play tunes on the keyboard: 'there must be more to it than that'. When asked about future plans this student teacher envisaged a teaching career of about fifteen years, after which he would study for a PhD. He wanted to avoid being stuck in a rut.

This scepticism was echoed in the reflections of the second male student, who had come to the conclusion that the aesthetic subjects were not essential to schools, because they could be experienced more directly and powerfully by young people outside the classroom. What he had gained however was a realisation 'that teaching involves working with children and building up relationships with them, which goes beyond merely talking about music'. This had led him to reassess his function: 'I shan't be teaching music, I shall be teaching children, and music is the medium through which I will be going to do it'. This was a significant shift of role identity. However his commitment was provisional, based upon whether he would be able to improve his teaching skills to his own satisfaction.

The remaining five female students expressed generally positive views about their experience, although their accounts are not unproblematic. For example, one individual found no problems as far as her teaching abilities were concerned, but felt vulnerable about her musical skills in the classroom. For others the experience changed perceptions about the nature of music in schools. Many had been attracted into music teaching by the extra-curricular activities, but now the work in the classroom demonstrated something important, 'that everyone is capable really, to a certain extent, of doing something in music, and it is a very valuable subject'.

It was a common experience that doubts arose at certain points in the teaching practice:

> I've spent years getting here. Can I still do it? I do find it very hard, and I wonder if that's because I want to do it so much that I get wound up about it when I feel that I can't.

But these doubts were generally resolved: 'I know it's the right thing now ... Towards the end I felt so comfortable doing it'.

There was one exception, a student who never wavered:

> I never wobbled ... I think it's a very hectic life where you have to be convinced by it ... it can't just be a money earner ... it has to be a genuine care for education, because of the work you have to put in after hours. But it's also incredibly rewarding.

Amongst this group of informants, the female students appeared more wholeheartedly committed to a teaching career than their more provisionally motivated male colleagues, an observation confirmed by Huberman (1993, 123-4) who notes the earlier and firmer career choices of female teachers. Mark (1999), in making a related point, draws on research which demonstrated that two-thirds of the pedagogically motivated music education students were female.

1.5 Summary

I have attempted to provide within a group biographical framework an overview of student teachers' prior musical experiences, as well as personal reflections on their own decisions to become both musicians and teachers. We have seen that the majority grew up in supportive homes, and were enouraged to learn a musical instrument. Nevertheless in general their parents were not highly musical. This could lead to a defensiveness by students about their musical background as they became more specialised. Schooling was a mixed experience, although membership of performing ensembles was highly valued. Some decided to enter teaching to emulate their own music teachers, whilst others were determined to counter their own negative experience. Finally, the impact of curriculum reforms appeared from their experiences to be patchy. Some schools were clearly implementing with enthusiasm the new emphasis upon composing and performing, whilst others appeared to take on only those developments that suited them. The early teaching experiences of these students underline the complexity of the task, and their varied responses to it. This brings us to the working lives of experienced music teachers.

2. Secondary School Music Teachers Talking

We know very little about the opinions or professional lives of teachers who teach music in secondary schools. This is unfortunate because there is a real problem with the recruitment (see Coll, 1998) and retention of secondary school music teachers. Music is the subject area in UK secondary schools with the biggest staff turnover and the greatest number of vacancies (Royal Society of Arts, 1995). However, the work of Hodge, Jupp and Taylor (1994) has illuminated our understanding of some aspects of music teachers' lives. They compared stress amongst music and mathematics teachers in Australia. It was established that music teachers taught a sizeable number of classes each week, coped with high amounts of practical work leading to increased noise levels in classrooms, experienced relative isolation in small departments, and felt marginalised as teachers of a 'practical' and 'non-academic' subject. The conclusion was that such factors could be expected to result in higher levels of stress and lower perceptions of personal accomplishment amongst music teachers, than for those in most other subject areas.

In this section I argue that more attention needs to be paid to the concerns of secondary school music teachers. I set out to explore the realities of their work 'of how it is, more than how it should be' (Hargreaves, 1997, 710) by listening to the narratives and professional life histories of a small sample of ten secondary school music teachers, all of whom worked as mentors on the PGCE course at Reading. Of the ten teachers, four were female and six were male. The majority had been teaching between 10 and 25 years and were heads of department. Their schools were all state run, and represented a mixture of mixed and single sex, selective and comprehensive schools. All were located in urban areas within the relatively affluent Home Counties.

First I shall consider their perceptions of the National Curriculum, and shall then focus on music teaching as a career, its intersections with the personal musical lives of the teachers, and the lows and highs of everyday music teaching. Finally I shall develop some ideas about re-defining the role of the secondary school teacher in today's schools.

2.1 Teaching Music in the National Curriculum

The subject specialism of secondary school teachers plays a crucial role in their personal identity (Ball and Goodson, 1985). The subject curriculum is at the heart of what they do, it serves as a definition of their work (see Connell, 1985). Since the introduction of the National Curriculum in 1992 however, teachers in state schools in the United Kingdom have had less freedom to develop their own curriculum. For music teachers in England this has meant having to focus on two main areas of connected work when teaching pupils between the ages of 5-14 for whom the subject is compulsory: Performing and Composing, Listening and Appraising.

Commentators have considered how the imposition of the National Curriculum has eroded the close relationship between teachers and what counts as knowledge in the school curriculum. Although generally there does appear to have been a possible decline in teacher autonomy, Helsby and McCulloch (1996) point out that there may be significant differences in the reactions of different groups of teachers to such initiatives.

It is my contention that music teachers comprise one of these significantly different groups. I found that the music teachers I interviewed did appear to have a generally positive view of the National Curriculum. There were two distinct opinions. On the one hand, Music in the National Curriculum was seen as an evolutionary step, whilst on the other hand it was regarded as an enormous change. Those who believed it was evolutionary, growing out of their previous practice felt confirmed in what they were doing:

> I liked it when it came in, because it was doing the things I was already doing ... they (the pupils) were already composing and performing, there was a range of listening work.

This meant that not much changed in classroom practice, 'it hasn't bothered the way we teach'. The teacher amplified this view:

> We have to look back occasionally and check we're not missing out certain things, but I think certainly at this school we do understand the spirit of it.

It is that insight which is crucial to music teacher perceptions, that the spirit informing the Music National Curriculum is on the right lines. The emphasis upon composing and performing means 'you are steered away from copious note writing and listening ... biographical accounts of composers'. Moreover it has offered teachers the chance to grow, providing opportunities for them to be focusing upon what 'they should really be delivering ... multi-cultural aspects, information technology'.

Some informants, however, found the change to the National Curriculum more radical, simply because it replaced a system which was *laissez-faire*:

> When I started teaching there was actually no structure at all ... The only information I had was the timetable on a piece of rough paper ... By the end of the first morning the head of department spoke to me about the fact that I taught a class a song they already knew, and now I look back on it and think 'how the hell was I supposed to know that?' So the National Curriculum was a vast improvement.

Its emphasis upon 'hands-on doing' was characterised by one teacher as a radical advance on previous practice.

But this largely positive view was not quite unanimous. One informant put it like this:

> I think people are so bogged down with legislation and have to do this and they have to do that ... And I think you have to be very careful ... It may be written down, is it actually appropriate? I think you have to be very careful not to stick

rigidly to it, because then you can lose yourself and your own identity, and your own love for the various subject areas within music.

There were varied opinions about music technology, which was becoming a priority in the new framework. Like the Music National Curriculum the ground in music technology had been prepared beforehand. The development of technology in music classrooms owes much to the Technical and Vocational Educational Initiative (TVEI) which commenced in 1984 as a four-year curriculum designed as a preparation for adult life in a rapidly changing society. Although starting off as narrowly vocational, it gradually came to embrace the arts (see Green, 1992). Funds were made available for music teachers to buy hardware. By 1987 music was placed by the Department of Education and Science (DES) at the top of the list of 'known strengths of computer technology in education' (ibid.). £10.5 million was earmarked for music education use.

Opinion was divided between those of my informants who felt highly positive about music technology, and those who had qualms. Amongst the latter there was often a degree of guilt: 'I'm ashamed to say I cannot expand much on that because I have not geared myself to'. Another teacher admitted weakness in that area, but explained it was due to a lack of pupil interest in working the computer. Technology became 'a new pressure' particularly when it had to be assessed. But it was the maintenance of the equipment which presented the greatest headaches: 'There's always something going wrong that needs to be fixed'. Nevertheless the same teacher admitted:

> It is a most useful aid at GCSE, that's where they really use the computer, for people who want to sequence and people who can't notate, or for some reason want to have their performance pre-recorded.

Others, however, have welcomed technology with open arms:

> For me that has been one of the really exciting things, because I have always had an interest in IT and I was able to develop a lot of my experience ... it was refreshing to go into the classroom and to be introduced to the power and potential of a very simple computer ... It is one aspect ... I've built up, because that is one aspect I get very excited about.

It is that welcoming of trying out new things that characterises such teachers. Pupils themselves provide an impetus and teach the teacher. In one instance a pupil helped build a studio. Strategies are developed that build on this:

> If I have a new CD-ROM or if I have a new software package of any kind, it's the children who will get to know it first before me, so very often and at the beginning

of a lesson I will say to them: ' Find out how to do this, and at the end of the lesson I'd like you to show the rest of the class' ... That way I'm learning and it saves me having to sit there for hours.

There are very few teachers however who see technology as the Saviour of music education:

It is just an additional resource ... The thing I really hate is those magazines ... from manufacturers and you see children sitting in rows, all with headphones on ... I think you lose that whole community thing if you are not careful.

Essentially technology is evolutionary according to this view:

You might sequence a piece, but that is not inherently different from giving the parts out to performers and performing it. You might print it out on a computer but that is not inherently different from writing it out by hand ... What it has done has made the recording and playing back of class work a viable possibility to a high quality ... I think that putting sound-producing means at the disposal of even the least able pupil has perhaps if not been revolutionary, it has added a dimension to what you can do in class.

Undoubtedly technology is seen as a way of engaging the interest of pupils, it has the potential to build on pupil expertise, and also develop the skills of the teacher. One of the characteristics of Gammon's (1996) model of good practice is to 'use technology, IT, as much as possible' (ibid., 113). However, Goodson and Mangan (1998) point out that the cultures of teaching are closely linked to the cultures of subjects, and that teachers often see an 'either/or' choice: either I can co-opt the computer to fit with what I am doing, or my practice can be overthrown. Encouragingly few of my informants subscribed to the latter view. A significant number identified technology as a way of transforming their practice.

Overall there seemed little doubt that the music teachers I interviewed were working comfortably within the National Curriculum. It might be argued that this apparent consensus is explained by the evolution of the National Curriculum model from the previous work of John Paynter, whose book *Sound and Silence* (Paynter and Aston, 1970) was frequently mentioned in conversation, and Keith Swanwick (1979). Certainly there was unanimity in the notion that music is a practical subject in which the central focus should be on composing and performing, listening and appraising. On the other hand the teachers may have perceived their subject to have been strengthened through its inclusion into the National Curriculum, its compulsory status regarded as a significant advance for what had often been regarded as an inessential subject. It is most likely that a combination of these factors influenced the positive view of the curriculum expressed by my informants.

2.2 *Music Teaching as a Career*

The picture became less positive when I considered music teachers' day to day lives. I specifically asked whether they would recommend some of their musically able pupils to think about teaching music as a career. More than half expressed considerable reservations. This led to searching reflections about the possibilities and drawbacks of teaching music.

Promotion within the school system was problematic because it depended increasingly on letting go of music. Some simply did not want further career progression: what attracted music teachers into teaching was music and 'the very special opportunities that music offers ... relating to pupils and putting things together and creating'. Even so this teacher characterised a career in music teaching as 'a total dead-end. You become a head of department and that's it ... Most people will get to their 40s and wonder whether this is what their whole life will be'. Trying to move out from music into senior management however was not easy, as 'music is seen as a little bit dead-endish'. This leads to frustration:

> People don't see you as a music teacher as being the right kind of person for those jobs, because they think you should be English or History or Maths.

At some point the realisation of the closing up of opportunities becomes a personal crossroads, and then the development of the right frame of mind becomes important:

> You really have to look and say 'what can the classroom offer me? and what can I get out of the classroom? and can I continue to make the career challenging and exciting day in and day out?' ... it is looking for small things to make them big and important ... so that you can never feel that you've arrived.

On the other hand, music teaching suited a female teacher because it combined a career with bringing up a family. She turned it to her own advantage, 'into a positive experience'.

In summary, these music teachers do not rate their chances of promotion within or outside the school very highly. They betray little bitterness about this, because teaching their subject is of most importance to them. There are similarities to Bennet's reporting of art teachers' attitudes to their careers (1985), which makes the point that the status hierarchy of school subjects disadvantages the so-called practical subjects. But the group of art teachers interviewed did not suffer from low morale but rather had the freedom of being both an artist and an art teacher. Bennet observed that satisfying involvement in both areas improved the quality of her informants' total career. Sikes, Measor and Woods (1985) and Sikes (1987) make a similar point. Art teachers are heavily committed to their subject above all else. Marginal status in a school may mean a special kind of freedom.

To what extent can we apply this to music teachers? Do they perceive themselves to be both musicians and music teachers?

2.3 Intersections

In my questioning I attempted to gauge the points of intersection between institutional roles and personal musical lives. Gammon (1996) has pointed out that a number of music teachers make a distinction between their dual status as trained musicians and music teachers, and develop distancing attitudes towards the latter. It was expressed like this by one of my informants:

> There are odd occasions when I simply don't want to listen to music ... I want to listen to music because I love music and I am interested and want to listen to something new or whatever, but not as a school teacher analysing it.

I found this uncharacteristic however. There was general agreement that an active musical life outside of school was desirable. Some teachers were active conductors and players, and believed the benefits paid off in terms of effective teaching: 'The pupils will pick up musicianship at a stroke'. This did not simply include performing but composing as well:

> It can be quite soul destroying if you are teaching pupils to compose all day long and you are not composing yourself ... one of the things I have enjoyed ... is to be able to compose incidental music ... for the school productions.

Nevertheless there was a tension between in-school and out-of-school music making for the music teacher. Priorities had to be made:

> I think that it is important that whatever you do outside, that you realise ... the fact that my teaching pays the mortgage ... I know there is a clash, but school stuff does come first.

This could lead to frustration, when parents' evenings and induction evenings meant orchestral playing had to be missed. Sometimes a teacher put her foot down:

> It's not liked at school ... it's like 'I'm very sorry but I have to play my violin' ... it's ridiculous I am apologising for my profession.

The dilemma was neatly expressed by another teacher:

> Education is an all-consuming at times unrewarding profession. You have to delicately balance your time, and make extreme sacrifices in order to sometimes progress your own ability.

I did not sense in my interviews the separation between the institutional and personal subject interests that I perceived in reading the research on art teachers. It appeared that one of the reasons that a musical life was pursued outside of school was that one's teaching might be more successful. There was little feeling that experienced music teachers longed to become professional musicians. The intersections between private and institutional roles seemed to be different for music teachers compared to art teachers. There appears to be a more single-minded commitment to the institution.

2.4 Lows and Highs

That commitment, however, was continually tested. Huberman (1993) has identified the classic motivations for going into teaching as the 'contact with young people' and 'love of subject matter'. Those provided the highs, and when they were contradicted, the lows.

The downside of teaching as might be expected was the wear and tear of classroom indiscipline. This is particularly difficult for most music teachers:

> In some respects you have to develop a thick skin, which is contrary to everything a musician stands for because they are ... normally very sensitive.

Sometimes earlier in a career this had led to extreme frustration:

> You think 'why am I here banging the piano lid and saying "I'm not having this"?' ... What you have to really do, is not to let it get to your soul ... but really to think it is not the most important thing in the world if you have not succeeded every moment of the day.

The disciplinary problems in another teacher's reminiscence had been exacerbated by inadequate resources:

> Poor resources, large classes, kids fighting amongst themselves and not behaving, you're exhausted and you feel 'I can't stand this any longer'.

All this was heightened by a clash of values, between the teacher's commitment and the attitudes from home:

I get very cross and very depressed when children don't have the same values as me, and don't treat the music as seriously as I would want them to treat it ... when boys won't sing because the dad says at home 'Oh that's sissy stuff', and you get these traditional home values coming through where the boys are expected not to be musical, but the girls are.

But the music teacher does not only have to keep classroom music functioning, there is the considerable pressure of maintaining and developing choirs, orchestras and other performing groups. This extra-curricular work, which presents the public face of the school to the community, frequently necessitates a large investment of the music teacher's time:

Not only do you have the lessons, but you have to work through your break, through your lunch, and work after school and then work weekends. It's not like teaching maths where you have a text book ... It's not an easy option.

The resulting intensification of teachers' lives, identified by Hargreaves (1997) as a common pressure caused by new initiatives and bureaucratic demands, was expressed like this:

I would say that in the last six or seven years my job has doubled in the number of hours that it requires ... I would estimate that it requires 65-70 hours a week of actual school work ... Because you tend to be head of a small department not much can be delegated, and you are responsible for a vast amount of extra-curricular work ... all the new reporting requirements, assessing requirements, marking your own exams ... that is a huge amount of work.

Because teaching music is so physically demanding being able to cope with stress was important. Achieving balance in one's life was seen to be crucial, having areas of personal investment outside the school, permitting the teacher to step back and relativise the problems that come up in the classroom (see Huberman, 1993):

I think it is important to have a life as well outside ... and if necessary if you've had a bad day, just go home, don't take any work home, watch the telly, go have a drink.

When asked about the rewards, the teachers generally focused on individual children, and the impact of their work on the school community:

When you see individual pupils first of all enthused by what you have done towards music and particularly those for whom you have given a completely fresh start. They would never have been involved in music if it had not been for you ... and to

see them progress and even to the extent ... they want to stay in touch ... that for
me is the greatest reward.

On other occasions it is the communal nature of making music together in the
classroom that provides the richest benefit:

It's also wonderful when I notice the less able children, when they have struggled
with something and then they perform it to the class and the class applauds, and
then you think 'Ah, they're actually feeling, they're sensitive ... they are all part
of a group together' ... it's the emotional side of things that I feel so strongly
about.

These communal occasions often focus on concerts and their intensive
preparation. For example a teacher refers to her steel band:

I'm actually considering taking them on tour next year because they're really
good and they just play. They play, like 20 songs through off by memory ... You
think 'yes, they're musical, they're playing by ear, they're listening to each other,
they don't actually need me'.

One is reminded here of Gammon's advice to student teachers, 'that the
ultimate aim of good music teachers should be to make themselves redundant'
(Gammon, 1996, 115).

Several of the music teachers testified to the considerable personal
satisfaction of shaping a job so that it becomes a reflection of one's own
identity, a result of professional commitment (see Hargreaves, 1997):

One of the senior teachers said 'the music in the school is you' and that was quite
nice because it was a reflection that everything that happened here, the energy
I've put in, the time I had put in and the gradual reputation over the many years
that I've built;

With music each person has their own style, and somebody else could not pretend
to do it like me, but you feel as if you have really got something from that.

The ultimate reward is that an individual music teacher can have a revitalising
effect on the whole school community:

You bring into a school something new, and you succeed to the point where the
school ... is renewed ... that's extremely exciting.

For several of my informants their overall contribution to the life of a school
became a personal symbol of their creativity, a means of defining themselves.

2.5 Discussion

Judging from the narratives quoted here, the inclusion of music teachers' own assessments of their experience enlarges our own understanding of the complexity underlying their day to day professional lives.

These experienced music teachers welcomed the challenge and opportunity afforded by the National Curriculum, largely because it was based on a practical hands-on approach with which they identified. But their career opportunities were seen as limited, and this produced frustration about the heavy workload and lack of official recognition in terms of promotion. The low status of music in schools was a constant theme. The pressures of long hours, large classes and coping with constant noise took their toll at particular times. But to counter this, there were the rewards of dealing with young people making music: this is what kept the group motivated. There was little evidence that these teachers longed to pursue a music career out of school. In many ways it was making music in school and thereby exercising a personal influence on the institution that seemed to be of most importance.

The central dilemma therefore is the tension between the personal investment that music teachers contribute to schools (in terms of workload, motivation of young people to make music, organisation of work inside and outside the curriculum), and the lack of recognition that music teachers receive in a career structure in which they are disadvantaged.

3. Conclusion

This chapter represents a first stage in giving voice to music teachers. Subsequent work will need to develop explanatory concepts arising from the teachers' interviews, including power, ideology and marginalisation, in order to make sense of music teachers' lives 'in the round' (see Green, 2000). This will also involve taking a more detached view of the significance of the categories that teachers identify as being significant in their own experience.

Essentially in the chapter I have attempted 'to look beyond the school house door' (Goodson, 1994, 51) in order to understand something of the internal nature of music in schools as experienced and felt by teachers and student teachers, because it is in schools that the reality of the curriculum is negotiated. In conclusion I draw together the main findings from both sets of interviews with secondary school music teachers, and student music teachers.

Running through the accounts there is a perception that involvement in music and music teaching is problematic. Because of their specialised training as musicians, some student teachers displayed a defensiveness about their musical backgrounds at home, which often did not 'fit' with their later definitions of what counted as music. Even when they were pupils at school, some of the student teachers found and resented the separation that occurred between themselves, and those of their peers who did not regard themselves as musicians. All this creates a potential distance between the trained musician who becomes a teacher and the majority of children s/he will teach. There were similar residual attitudes amongst some of the secondary school music teachers, who perceived tensions within themselves in their joint roles as musicians and as school teachers.

There is no doubt that the teaching of music in schools is problematic. Most of the student teachers' experiences of being taught music were mixed and uneven. Some testified to its sheer tedium and predictability. What is disappointing is the apparent lack of impact of the curriculum development music projects of the 1970s on the classroom experiences of these students when at school. As we have seen in the previous chapter, such curriculum development motivated many music teachers. This does not appear to guarantee a lasting influence upon classroom practice however. There is a warning light here: the apparent satisfaction expressed by present-day music teachers concerning the Music National Curriculum may not be automatically shared by their pupils.

The music teachers point to some of the issues which make for difficulty in making the teaching of the subject effective, most of which stem from the subject's low status within schools. A significant proportion were reluctant to recommend the job to others. When student teachers undertook their own teaching it challenged their commitment severely.

All this must be balanced by the occasional inspirational moments to which students testify: the contact with a particularly effective music teacher; the sheer joy in discovering an ability to compose; the profound satisfaction in performing music with others both inside and outside school. Music teachers too have moments which give them rewards: the chance to make music communally; the emotional satisfaction of seeing children of different abilities perform side by side; the creation of a musical environment within the school which reflects their personal contribution.

The question which looms here, however, is whether music can really function effectively within the institutional constraints of formal schooling. Swanwick (1999) sums up the position succinctly by highlighting the disconnection between school music and 'real' music:

> No wonder 'school music' appears to many young people as a sub-culture separated from music out there in the world, abstracted by the constraints of classroom and curriculum ... We have to do better than this. (Ibid., 100)

It brings us back to the question posed in the first chapter of this book: how can one teacher in every single school hope to encompass the metaphorical richness of the genuine musical experience in his/her teaching? How can we reform and transform the process of teaching music in schools so that it becomes connected with 'real' instruments, 'real' music, 'real' musicians and 'real' music making sessions ? (ibid.). The question has resonated throughout the historical contexts explored in this book. Towards the end of my next and final chapter I attempt to propose ways forward, ways of doing 'better than this'.

7 Conclusion

As a preface to this chapter I would like to draw the reader's attention to the work of Ivor Goodson, the curriculum historian, which I have found illuminating during the writing of this book. It provides a basis for my own conclusions.

His point is that curriculum theory has developed an amnesia concerning the historical past (see Goodson and Marsh, 1996, 1). On the contrary however, it is this sense of historical perspective that could make all the difference in our understanding of the curriculum, and the positioning of subjects within it. The problem is that the curriculum is generally regarded as a given, something natural and immutable. But Goodson argues that it is a social artefact, an archetype of 'the division and fragmentation of knowledge within our societies' (ibid., 150). By studying the history of school subjects we come to realise they are 'the most quintessential of social and political constructions' (ibid., 1).

The purpose of studying the curriculum is not arcane however, but severely practical: to understand the past as context for the present. Through historical reflection we can gain the potentiality for transforming our understanding, posing fundamental problems and pointing to new agendas of study (Goodson, 1985, 363)).

Similarly in the writing of this book I have been concerned about how the music curriculum has been formulated, and how it has been enacted. I have focused through a historical lens on attempts to improve the quality of music education within our schools, with the intention of relating the past to the present. In the discussion that follows I have isolated, what seem to me, three important areas of discussion which consolidate aspects of this history: the rhetorical discourse about music as a school subject; stages of curriculum change in music; living music in schools in the future.

1. Rhetorical Discourse about the Place of Music in the Curriculum

There is little doubt that both in the UK and the USA more attention has been paid by historians to the scrutiny of recommendations and suggestions for what should be taught, than for what in reality is taught: what Labaree calls the 'rhetorical curriculum' (in Franklin, 1999, 463). Subjects like music which have to fight for their existence on the curriculum are particularly prone to soul-searching debates about justification.

What arises from my account is that the 75 years or so under consideration have witnessed struggles between groups representing different conceptions of what musical experiences should be embodied in the curriculum, and to what ends the curriculum in music should be directed. Drawing on Kliebard (1995) we might characterise the groups as follows. First, the humanists, the keepers of the tradition, tied to the finest elements of the western canon, and committed to the traditional skills that were associated with it. Second, the developmentalists, committed to a curriculum in harmony with children's real interests. Third, the social meliorists, who maintain that schools act as major forces for social change and social justice. Fourth, the advocates of social efficiency, who believed that social utility was the supreme criterion against which the value of school subjects was measured.

Of course these categories are not exclusive. We recognise the humanist tradition in the constant concern about the teaching of basic musical skills, particularly musical notation. But there have been constant shifts in this position. For example, in the 1920s the teaching of sight reading through the use of the voice was the prevailing orthodoxy, whilst in the 1940s music educators were advocating sight reading using instruments. It was the work of Bentley *et al* in the Schools Council Project 'Music Education of Young Children' that attempted to revitalise the teaching of traditional musical skills in primary schools, utilising tape recordings so that children could work on an individual or paired basis for some of the time. However, that particular project appeared to be swimming against the tide. The development of new approaches focusing upon creative music in the 1970s were perceived as a threat to such traditional concerns, yet for Odam and Salaman at least, the teaching of music literacy was still central in the next decade. By the 1990s the letters to *The Times Educational Supplement* re-emphasised concerns about the necessity of teaching musical literacy, and getting back to a more orthodox position.

But this humanist tradition has always been pre-eminent because it is intimately connected with academic status. One of the constant themes of Goodson and Marsh (1996), is the aspirational imperative to become an academic subject, as McLaren (in Goodson, 1993, xxi) exclaims, 'the academic tradition holds all the cards'. This is a problem for a subject like music. Certainly its place as a matriculation subject was hard fought, and schools like Mary Datchelor in the 1920s reaped considerable benefits from music's increased academic status. The problem was that pressing the subject into such a mould could distort it, so that it could be a disembodied shadow of itself, which in many ways was the case in the post-war GCE 'O' level examinations. In parenthesis, the York project's powerful influence on the GCSE did much to redeem this situation.

But behind the rhetorical facade of the humanist tradition in music education lies the pre-active definitions and constructions of the subject before it enters the classroom. And here we come across one of the central problems with music. Goodson (1988) points to the crucial work of Vulliamy in this respect in the 1970s. Vulliamy asked what counted as music in school, and found a rigid stratification between the popular and classical genres. Goodson asks: 'what sort of mass education is being pursued when that which is popular is not merely ignored but positively disvalued?' (ibid., 20). Music finds itself on the horns of a dilemma, between providing music for the majority on the one hand, and for the musically talented on the other. The humanist tradition appears to have more to say to pupils in the latter category and sits uneasily alongside the pluralist culture which the majority of pupils inhabit. It seems that music is caught in between.

Much of the talk about the belief in music as a 'spiritual' or 'divine' force was being expressed at the start and end of our chronological survey and in many ways is connected with the humanist tradition centred on the transcendence of music. One of the most recent examples can be found at the end of McCarthy's (1999) study of Irish formal and informal music education, in which she calls for the creation of a democratic and dynamic system of music education, a task which 'is fundamentally a spiritual one - connecting the generations through the at-once mystical and tangible phenomenon of music' (ibid., 195). Ideas like this have permeated the justifications and aims of music education.

But such statements extend beyond a simply humanist position, they also connect with social meliorism, in which music is believed to possess the power to regenerate society. After all, if music is so elemental and fundamental there is no limit to its power. Walford Davies's conviction in 1923 that melody was 'our mother-tongue', connects with Everitt's assertion in 1998 that music was 'our primary language', which in turn reinforced the belief, articulated by Hunt in 1948, that it had the power to effect a refining influence on young people's life. Music, far from being on the periphery of the curriculum, might be expected, according to *The 4th 'R' Report* in 1998, to play a key role in a pupil's performance in other subjects.

The social meliorist tradition was central to Walford Davies's belief in the importance of 'fellowship', in which music could play a central role. Such thinking has comprised a crucial strand in justifying music in the curriculum, exemplified today in much talk about community music, and Swanwick's (1999) dream of harnessing the 'musical richness beyond the school gates'. We should bear in mind however that the relation between music and social change is complex, and needs to take into account notions of power and resistance.

The countervailing position to that of the humanists was taken by the developmentalists, and to a certain extent was connected with the central notion shared by MacPherson and Swanwick in the 1920s and 1970s, of music as 'aesthetic' education. It entailed music education moving away from extrinsic outcomes to an emphasis on pupils encountering music on its own terms, and on their own terms. Thus music was able to become self-enriching through the ability it engendered to perceive and feel. In turn this connected with de Rusette's conviction, stated in 1948, in the importance of children expressing themselves through music according to their own powers of observation and experience: children could form their own 'little creative heaven of sound' (Davies in 1923). The work of Musical Education of the Under-Twelves achieved much in thinking about and practically promoting the notion of the value of children's musical and creative impulses. The culmination of this approach in the 1970s with the Schools Council Project 'Music in the Secondary School Curriculum' and its alliance with radical approaches from the avant-garde and popular music gave rise to much soul searching, and represented a climactic and defining moment in the history of music education.

Finally, we should note the recent appearance of advocates of social efficiency in our education system. They subscribe to a science of exact measurement and precise standards and to a direct connection between what is taught in schools and the adult activities individuals would play as adult members of the social order. In many ways the New Labour government illustrates this tendency in its determination to prioritise 'the basics' of literacy and numeracy, and to justify its stance by appealing to the measurement of results. It was this social efficiency philosophy that was one of the causes of the jolt that music educators received in 1998, when music had to fight for its life for a place on the school curriculum.

2. Stages of Curriculum Change in Music

There has been no shortage of curriculum innovations during these years. The development of different technologies has frequently propelled these, ranging from the wireless, gramophone, film, to 'classroom instruments' and ICT. But again we note continuities between the percussion bands of the 1940s and the classroom orchestras of the 1970s, between MacPherson's pioneering work on appreciation in the 1920s, and Peggie's plea for a return to such work in the 1990s.

I find it helpful to reflect on such changes and continuities by considering a four-stage process of curriculum change, looked at as a socio-political process: invention, promotion, legislation, mythologisation (see Goodson and Marsh 1996, 144-6).

The invention of curriculum ideas is complex, and is linked, according to Goodson and Marsh, with the ideas of educators, the climate of opinion and pupil demands. Certainly in this account there have been key individuals who have been responsible for developing curriculum ideas including Arnold Bentley, Kathleen Blocksidge, Walford Davies, Ann Driver, Stewart

MacPherson, and John Paynter. To what extent these individuals were influenced by the climate of opinion is not clear, often they flew in the face of it. For example, Walford Davies's ideas about tune building were developed in the teeth of opposition, and both Paynter and Bentley thought the time was not right for either of their diametrically opposed projects. Certainly MEUT was a victim of the changing educational climate between the publication of the Plowden Report in 1968, and the appearance of the first of the Black Papers in the following year.

Sometimes our innovators saw their solutions in almost messianic terms. Walford Davies proclaimed that the alliance of music education and broadcasting could change the face of music in schools. Proponents of the York Project frequently argued that the time was ripe for a break with past tradition, in which curriculum history could be transcended. It is apposite to recall that the golden age of such thinking was between 1960 and 1975, the era of the rise of the comprehensive school and of economic expansion, and that in spite of the rhetoric and good intentions, generally speaking, radical change did not occur (see Goodson, Anstead and Mangan, 1998, 13). Similarly, educational broadcasting found it difficult to live up to Walford Davies's dreams.

As for curriculum change being prompted by pupil demands, the York project is a valuable example, its birth being fertilised as it was by the opinions of young school leavers, mediated through the Newsom Report and the Schools Council *Enquiry One*. However this was two-edged. On the one hand the reports provided the project with a good deal of relevance in meeting the needs of educationally disaffected young people, but on the other hand, as Goodson and Marsh (1996, 44) point out, subject status is invariably skewed towards the academic tradition, whilst progressive ideas have frequently been applied to pupils of comparatively low status. This conjunction in the York Project may in retrospect have had a negative influence on the subsequent standing of music in the curriculum.

Goodson's second stage of curriculum change is promotion. Music education has certainly never been short of evangelists to further the cause in alliance with others. Walford Davies, for example, was able to find a perfect vehicle in the school broadcast, and a powerful sphere of influence within the BBC. Bentley's and Paynter's work with the Schools Council had considerable potential to promote the cause, although the mixed messages that resulted were counter-productive. Finally, the creation of MEUT as an umbrella organisation which might help promote a unity across the different factions within music education, can be regarded as a valiant grassroots attempt to transmit a strong message, even although it ultimately died.

Goodson points out that subjects with low status, poor career patterns and survival problems may come to readily embrace new inventions within and across subjects as a means of promoting themselves. Music might be seen as one such subject. However, for good or ill, music educators were not prepared to compromise what they saw as the integrity of the subject. One of the most illuminating moments in this connection, was the hostility shown by the Schools Council Music Committee to proposals from 'The Arts and the Adolescent' project as well as to the considerable doubts the committee expressed about integrated arts work. If music was seen to be at risk, these alliances might be seen as potentially life saving. To the contrary however, the committee's rejection of such advances was complete. Whether this was the result of sheer confidence in music's future as a curriculum subject, or a defensiveness and fear of contamination is worthy of further investigation.

I have adopted a fairly broad view of the third stage of curriculum change, legislation, to encompass publications emanating from government containing advice, and suggestions about music teaching. These comprise a solid tradition extending from the *Handbook of Suggestions* (1937), *Music in Schools* (1956, 1969), *Creative Music in Education* (1970), *Music 5-16* (1985). These were helpful barometers of opinion, and certainly in the first three examples provided 'top-down' advice from HMI, based upon their knowledge of what was happening in schools. They were generally supportive of teachers, and helped provide a loose sense of coherence in a context in which teachers possessed considerable freedom.

This brings us to Goodson's fourth stage of curriculum change, which is best exemplified by the National Curriculum. Mythologisation refers to the fact that once automatic support has been achieved for a subject, a fairly wide range of activities can be undertaken. The music guidelines were felt to be flexible enough to encompass much teaching that had been developing since the 1960s. Consequently teachers generally felt it was evolutionary, growing out of their previous practice. The current emphasis upon classroom composition in groups is an example of a taken for granted activity which now dominates classrooms.

However, such developments as the Music National Curriculum, the Schools Council music projects, the BBC school music broadcasts, tend to fix the form and content of the music curriculum which then becomes accepted without question by the majority of teachers with little or no reference to historical perspectives. But Goodson (1994) suggests that to make sense of the process of curriculum change we might adopt Hobsbawm's notion of the 'invented tradition' (see Hobsbawm and Ranger, 1983). The music curriculum is frequently mythologised according to custom. We have seen how the humanists have been regarded as the keepers of tradition, keen to defend their territory against the onslaughts of newfangled innovations. But if we regard the written curriculum, whether in the form of courses of study, textbooks, syllabuses or guidelines, as a supreme example of the invention of tradition, we can start to unpick the mystifications. Part of this process includes a revitalisation of our historical understanding concerning the formation of the curriculum.

3. Living Music in Schools in the Future

The status of a school subject is crucial, linked as it is to the material and self interests of teachers. The way a teacher is able to teach music effectively in school is inseparable from such a concern. Music teachers are in the front line of the battle to establish the credentials of their subject, and this entails conflict over status, resources and territory. One of the themes running throughout the narrative has been the provision of proper training as the key to enhanced professionalism. But the lack of such a training for primary school teachers who wish to teach music has been a constant cause for concern. This has meant that the musical quality of the teaching has been, to say the least, variable. It is a vicious circle, leading to music teachers being less than enthusiastic to recommend the job to others. The key element in this lack of endorsement appears to be the weakness of an adequate career structure for music teachers, which is closely linked with such issues as isolation and poor resources.

Unfortunately music's status as a curriculum subject is ambivalent. On the one hand it has an ancient and distinguished educational pedigree, forming part of the mediaeval and renaissance *quadrivium* based upon its intellectual rigour, on the other hand it is frequently regarded as a piece of educational frippery, associated with leisure and mass media manipulation.

But subject status is not fixed. In many ways it depends upon how the subject can cope with the profound changes that occur in society. One of these profound changes lies in the sheer accessibility of music today. Music teachers find themselves working in a challenging environment in which we are 'Drowning in Music', the title of a provocative article by Joseph Bottum (2000) in the *New Statesman*. Bottum rails against the way music permeates almost everything we do. He argues that with the rise of recorded music people first began to imagine that morality was a set of feelings rather than a system of ideas: they could evoke any mood by putting a record on the gramophone. Today, sheer accessibility has created our musical problem.

This has come about with a decline in the intellectual coherence of human beings and the world, so that whilst we may have an endlessly expanding library of music, the enormous width is obscured by the shallow depth. Thus Bottum calls music 'chess drenched with perfume', at once the most rigorous and the least rigorous of the arts: our breadth of musical knowledge has been gained at the expense of depth of musical emotion. Bottum's conclusion is that 'adrift on a sea of sound', music today is in the way, keeping us from finding a purpose for 'our all-encircling noise'.

I have selected Bottum's piece because it encapsulates a challenge that has permeated music education from the time the first recording techniques entered the classroom through the radio and gramophone, and is now more than ever a dilemma with related developments in ICT and the internet: how to cope with the awful popularity of music, and still be able to induct young people into its mysteries and its possibilities. A successful response by music educators might help to raise the subject's status.

Anthony Everitt's report *Joining In* (1997) provides a helpful summation of the state of participatory music in the UK in the 1990s. Underlying all the shifts in musical behaviour that Everitt catalogues is massive social change, transforming our ways of living. The old idea of community is being replaced by individualism and the emergence of relative value systems. The increased accessibility of recorded music has meant that consumption has become private rather than social. Front rooms have come to be the equivalent of the old arts centres. The sheer variety of music available on demand has brought a library of classical and popular music to all. A personal eclecticism is the result: 'People's timetables are now an *à la carte* menu rather than the old familial and collective *table d'hôte*' (ibid., 22).

For Theberge (1993) electronic culture is the pre-condition for contemporary musical culture. He focuses upon the significant impact of tape recording in the 1960s and early 1970s. First, multi-track recording in popular music production transformed the validity of past notions of musical composition and created new discontinuities in time and space. Second, the production during the 1970s of inexpensive portable cassette players achieved an unprecedented diffusion throughout the world, becoming the basis for an emergent world-wide popular music culture, whilst also playing a part in the survival of local, regional and national musical styles. Samplers and digital recording systems make sonic tours of exotic places easier, and results in a new genre of 'transcultural music' which has no clear origin within one particular ethnic group. All this facilitates what Theberge calls 'random access culture' (ibid., 161).

How are music teachers to cope with these fundamental changes? Will their endeavours result in a more genuinely musical experience being offered pupils in school? Everitt (1997) sees that with the decline of music making in the home, schools have an essential role in providing children with their first introduction to singing and playing instruments. In his opinion the Music National Curriculum could revolutionise not only music teaching, but also the quality of musical life in our society. Certainly schools are identified as the places where a complete cross-section of the population has access to the musical potential of the new technology. However, Everitt has some reservations. In reality music teachers are ill-equipped and ill-trained, there are too few of them, and in any case many schools remain unconvinced about the purposes of music in education.

In a reaction to the crisis of confidence in secondary school music teaching partly triggered by reports of its under-performance (see Mills, 1997), Swanwick (1997) has argued 'we have to think radically abut the future'. He suggests music teachers ought to be seen as professional musicians, a community resource, whose strengths would be capitalised upon through a radical look at the conventions of the timetable. The musical expertise of local music teachers would be pooled, they would teach to their strengths in activities which pupils would elect to join. The division between curricular and extra-curricular music would be eroded, and 'the musical richness beyond the school gates' (ibid.) would be harnessed.

George Odam (2000) suggests a different solution in his 'Creative Dream' project funded by Yamaha/Kemble Music (UK). This set out to identify good and effective teaching of composing in secondary schools. The 'dream' is to continue to find composing at the heart of music education. He pays tribute to the establishment of composing as a unique feature of the music curriculum in the United Kingdom, but is critical of the reliance on the small group format. The development of ICT in the music room may be one of the most significant areas which will effect change. But the message for music teachers is uncompromising:

> There is an urgent need for all music teachers to become computer literate. It is no longer acceptable to rely on pupils knowing more than the teacher does. (Ibid., 116)

The very different solutions of Swanwick and Odam have clear historical resonances extending back from Paynter to Walford Davies. Yet although there are continuities there are also discontinuities which may make all the difference to providing an enhanced status for music as a school subject.

Of course such a debate is not limited to the United Kingdom. In the USA during 1999 the Music Educators National Conference (MENC) addressed the profound changes that were occurring in music education, and published in the report *Vision 2020* (Madsen, 2000). Much of it is familiar. In her contribution to the debate Cornelia Yarborough (2000) identified the most important issues for music education in the twenty-first century as wider choices for schooling, ethnic and music diversity, the impact of technology and the digital revolution, and new approaches to teaching and learning. However, although we should be excited about the new possibilities, music educators need not be overwhelmed by techno-utopianism. As Yarborough points out, there will be a greater societal need for socialisation, and participation in music learning activities will become an important need to interact with one another in a social and educational setting.

Carletta Spearman (2000) asked 'How will societal and technological changes affect the teaching of Music?' Three implications appear paramount to her: responding powerfully to the possibilities of the technological revolution, devising more flexible school timetables to allow for quality instruction, and developing community partnerships with music education to provide for people of all ages which may cause a relocation of 'where music teaching happens' and the forms it will take.

In the light of all this we may conclude that those within the music education profession, whether experienced music teachers, new entrants to the profession, or teacher trainers, need to be ready to re-define roles, and to be proactive in suggesting fresh ways of working which will enhance the musical experience of young people, and revitalise ourselves as teachers and musicians. Perhaps we need to locate our radical thinking within the perspective of the wider debate about the changing nature of teachers' work and culture in the post-modern age, in which Hargreaves (1994) observes the disjunction which comes about when society changes, but the basic structures of teaching and schooling do not. All of us who work within the music education community may soon be required to devise a radical solution to this dilemma.

Historical studies in music education comprise one set of weapons in the music teacher's armoury that may increase the effectiveness of living music in schools, through a greater awareness of past and present attempts to make music a powerful and vibrant presence within them. Living as we do in the midst of a musical revolution, more than ever we need a historical perspective to help make sense of it all. In particular the challenge to generate a present-minded history is urgent, but also immensely exciting, so that through the process of engaging with policy and practice we may be able to develop the powerful vision of a usable past. Music provides historians of education with a relatively unexplored space, through which we can better understand the cultural lives of young people, and at the same time exert some pressure on schools and communities to develop a music education which really can make a difference.

Afterword: Towards a Usable Past for Music Educators

This book has contained a number of stories about music educators and their attempts to establish a firm place for music in the school curriculum in the United Kingdom during the twentieth century. The purpose of this Afterword is to orientate the study within a wider context, with the intention of drawing the reader's attention to what I called, in the opening chapter, the potential richness of music education's history.

At this point we need to remind ourselves that the discipline of the history of music education is still emerging and is fragile, rather like the social history of music. During a coffee break at a conference, Dave Russell, author of *Popular Music in England 1840-1914* (1987), relates that

> I described myself to a new acquaintance as a 'social historian of music'. He replied that he was glad to meet me as he now knew all four of us. (Russell, 1993, 3)

The joke for Russell highlighted what he saw as the essentially submerged and inchoate nature of work in his field, frequently marginalised by both historians and musicians.

It might be argued that we are inheritors of a stronger tradition in music education if we think of three writers in particular. Percy Scholes' (1935) chronicle of the music appreciation movement and his two substantial sections covering the sight-singing century and music in the country's schools in *The Mirror of Music* (1947) are still essential reading for any self-respecting researcher interested in the development of nineteenth- and twentieth-century music education. Kenneth Simpson's edited collection *Some Great Music Educators* (1976) has served as a basic text for music education students for many years, and also contains an exposition of his views about the study of history in a chapter entitled 'The Antiquity of Modern Ideas'. And finally there is the work of Bernarr Rainbow (1914-1998) who almost single-handedly kept the flame of historical research in music education alight, from the publication of *The Land Without Music* (1967) to *Music in Educational Thought and Practice* (1989) which is a *tour de force* in its sheer breadth of coverage from the Ancient Greeks to the present day. Researchers in the field owe him an incalculable debt for his publication of source materials, *Classic*

Texts in Music Education (see Rainbow 1990), each of which contains a succinct and perceptive introduction setting the material in its context, and appraising its significance.

In spite of these landmarks, however, there is a concern shared with our colleagues in the social history of music, that much of the work that has been done has been marginalised. If we take the most representative academic journal in the field in the United Kingdom, *History of Education*, we find that only four articles dealing with music education have been published in 28 years (Lawrence, 1985; Allsobrook, 1990; Cox, 1996; Cox, 1999).

It is within this context of neglect that I shall present an overview of work undertaken within the field of the history of music education. I shall highlight some of the key texts, and to do this I have drawn on scattered material over a wider chronological span than the rest of the book. This has enabled me to identify a number of overarching themes which I shall develop and extend.

In particular I shall pursue four lines of enquiry. Firstly, to outline a digest of concerns within the parent discipline, the History of Education, in order to provide a sense of perspective. Second, to tease out some of the ideological assumptions that underpin established historical studies in music education. I shall demonstrate that these studies are characterised by celebratory accounts of a supposedly golden age of sight-singing instruction. Third, in the light of this somewhat restricted research tradition, to develop a broader view of what counts as music education. To illustrate the possibilities I shall bring together research dealing with local case studies of music teaching, music teachers, instructional materials, and interactions between music education, class and culture. Fourth, and most crucially, to develop the idea of a usable past for music educators, through researchers engaging with the current concerns of teachers and policy makers. This final section contains the heart of the matter.

1. Issues in the History of Education

What were the principal characteristics of research in the history of education in the first half of the twentieth century? Gordon and Szreter (1989) identify a trio of criticisms. First there was an excessive emphasis upon thinkers and writers, with little substantial reference to the period or the environment. More specifically there was a failure to explore the gap between noble, elevated schemes and the actual educational realities of the day.

Second, there was overmuch concern with the passing of educational legislation, rather than with issues arising out from it such as timing, adequacy or ideological hue. The approach tended to be 'Whiggist', celebratory in style, depicting public education as a continuous process, beneficial to all. Third, too much stress was placed upon the history of institutions, frequently uncritical and eulogistic in tone, which deflected attention away from agencies of informal education.

Such work lacked sufficient breadth of interest and tended to treat education as a closed system. Asa Briggs (1972) called for a history of education that could be considered as part of a wider history of society. More specifically Harold Silver (1983) argued that historians should see education 'not just "in context" ... but in society, as something of society, as forming and being formed by society' (ibid., 30). However, educational and social historians may have different priorities. Cunningham (1989) points out that the former tend to be rooted practically and institutionally in pedagogical concerns, whilst the latter are preoccupied when dealing with education with questions of cultural reproduction and social control.

Today, according to Richardson (1999), although the history of education still remains essentially conservative in its emphasis upon political and administrative history, there are new ideas emerging, particularly dealing with the education of women, and the history of the teaching profession.

These views and trends provide us with some critical yardsticks by which to assess work within the history of music education.

2. Bernarr Rainbow and *The Land Without Music*

The Land Without Music (Rainbow, 1967) is a landmark study in the history of music education and is representative of Rainbow's work. It was written within the comparative historical tradition of Pollard's book, *Pioneers of Popular Education* (1956). Its sub-title outlines its subject: 'Musical Education in England 1800-1860 and its Continental Antecedents'. Rainbow wrote out of pedagogical concerns: he wanted to find out why English achievements in the teaching of singing at sight came to be supplanted by continental methods until the arrival of John Curwen who synthesised the different strands (see Rainbow, 1980).

On closer examination it can be argued that the book was a justification for Rainbow's aesthetic, political and educational outlook. It is essentially whiggish although he looked back to a golden age of sight singing and hand signs that in reality probably never existed. In effect he treated sight-singing texts like 'company master plans' (see Colls, 1976). It was taken for granted that the development of an effective method would reap untold benefits upon popular music education. As part of this process the indigenous culture is portrayed as being deprived in some way:

> The dearth of musical experience afforded the rural populations in the first half of the nineteenth century is a staggering conception. (Rainbow, 1967, 37)

Rainbow regarded folk song as problematic because its musical characteristics did not fit the educational methods of such a well-known teacher as W.E. Hickson (see Hickson 1836):

casual acquaintance with the characteristic modal idiom of such folk songs as they heard would not have helped Hickson's rustic children to develop automatic mastery of the diatonic scale. (Rainbow, 1967, 38)

Furthermore, there is little detail from Rainbow's account of the teachers or pupils who used these instructional texts.

Rainbow was revealingly explicit about his historical beliefs in a paper entitled 'That Great Dust-Heap Called "History"' (1993). He allied himself with G.M. Trevelyan's romantic view of the poetry of history, and of history as a form of literature. The two key words which he used in opposition were 'civilisation' and 'liberalism'. What he termed our 'maladroit attempts at liberalisation' (ibid., 15) he appeared to connect in an earlier paper (Rainbow, 1985) with the development of popular music in the curriculum, the rise of creative music making in the classroom, the all-ability comprehensive school, and progressive methods of primary school teaching. In many ways the work of Kenneth Simpson, in his popular edited collection *Some Great Music Educators* (1976) reflected similar ways of writing history.

The work of Rainbow and Simpson might be characterised as follows: the creation of celebratory accounts of a rose-tinted past, specifically focusing on the contribution of John Curwen and the teaching of sight singing through tonic sol-fa, which resulted in a disengagement with contemporary culture; a concentration on formal music instruction, discounting informal methods; an emphasis upon leading educational figures, discounting the day-to-day experience of teachers and the children they taught.

3. Broadening Horizons

To face up to the implications of these critiques I shall next consider some selected accounts of work which reflect three concerns: that the research should be responsive to the social and historical contexts in which the teaching and learning of music take place; that due attention should be paid to the actual practice of music teaching and learning; that music education should be regarded as a broad area of activity encompassing both formal and informal settings.

I have chosen four themes to amplify these concerns: local histories of music instruction; images of music teachers; pedagogical texts; the relation of music education to social and cultural identity.

3.1 Localised Studies of Music Instruction

Local history according to Asa Briggs (1972) is basic to the understanding of the nature of education in the United Kingdom because of the 'localism' of the traditional British pattern. Such work, Briggs argued, needs to be more than a study of personalities and institutions, it should take into account structures and processes.

Localised studies of music instruction are sparse (however, see Button, 1989, and Cox, 1998), but a ground-breaking work was Nettel's *Music in the Five Towns 1840-1914* (1944). We see from the sub-title, its sphere of interest, 'A Study of the Social Influence of Music in an Industrial District'. The strength of the book lies in its focus upon the five townships comprising Stoke-on-Trent, shaped by the potteries, the mining industries, and Primitive Methodism. This brand of religion encouraged democratic forms of participation, and incorporated powerful, congregational singing as part of its evangelical drive. Music and its instruction were highly prized. Nettel provides us with a finely detailed account of local choirs and their teachers, and the pervading influence of musical competitive festivals in the lives of these communities. Essential to his analysis are the influences of geography and culture which give rise to different musical traditions within adjacent communities. For example Nettel compares the different reputations and styles of the pottery workers' Hanley Glee and Madrigal Society, with the miners' North Staffordshire District Choral Society. Nettel had a sympathy for 'the common man', and he suggested musical education might be proceeding in the wrong direction:

> The case for musical education of the masses has been too glibly twisted to mean the music that the individual musician thinks is suitable for the masses. It is all wrong. The test of suitability of music is the test of sincerity, and I for one would rather hear a man sing 'The Red Flag' because he feels that way than I would hear him try to sing the songs of Hugo Wolf because Ernest Newman says they are good for him. (Ibid., 45)

This concentration on 'history from below' and on a culturally diverse music curriculum was much ahead of its time within music education.

The overriding importance of geographical factors we have noted in *Music in the Five Towns* is central to Marsden's (1991) history of the Fleet Road Board School, Hampstead, between 1879 and 1903. He concentrates particularly on territorial segregation, perceptions and stereotyping of neighbourhoods which made up the school's catchment area. The school was located in the midst of the burgeoning piano factories of Kentish Town, with the huge factory of Brinsmead's playing a dominant role. Skilled piano makers had artisan élite status. Not surprisingly perhaps, music had a particularly high profile in the school whose prime purpose, according to Marsden, was the education of the respectable, aimed at children from the lower-middle and upper-working classes. In fact he develops a thesis that such groupings as school choirs were regarded with suspicion by the old-established Hampstead middle class, as they were instrumental in dismantling social barriers. Board school children, it was argued needed 'really useful training for manual labour' in order to supply the need for 'capable cooks, housemaids, general servants, or skilful and industrious workmen' (ibid., 239).

Marsden pinpoints the achievements of the school's infant teacher, Louisa Walker, who was nationally known for action song publications and her work with Froebelian action songs and games in the classroom. His point is, that like Louisa Walker, there are countless other teachers working in a local context with national reputations, whose lives have yet to be illuminated. Marsden also traces the work of the school's prestigious choir, its repertoire, and its trainer Jesse Harris, who suffered from the stress and pressure of the ubiquitous musical competitions which dominated extra-curricular work.

What these studies focusing on local contexts share, is a desire to explore the realities of music instruction through the perspectives of time, place and society. We thus gain a greater sense of the immediacy and the complexity of the processes of teaching and learning music through the lived experience of individuals, groups and communities in both formal and informal education.

In what ways might such work be extended? The problem is, as Humphreys (1997) has observed in the American context, that music education historians are invariably classically trained and study 'what fits into their conceptions of what should have been, rather than what was, and to underrepresent or ignore the rest' (ibid., 8). He provides some examples of neglect:

> Music education historians have written a great deal about the early orchestras, mixed choirs and bands, but have virtually ignored the huge numbers of glee clubs, harmonica bands, accordion and mandolin orchestras, guitar ensembles and athletic bands. (Ibid.)

Ruth Finnegan's study *The Hidden Musicians* (1989) might provide us with a model. She constructs an ethnography of amateur music making in Milton Keynes. Historians of music education can learn something from the inclusiveness of her coverage of the total musical environment incorporating brass bands, country and western clubs, rock bands, orchestras and classrooms.

This broadening of horizons brings new possibilities. There are intriguing areas of research hinted at by Gammon and Gammon (2000) concerning the traditional learning styles within brass bands, by Dunn (1980) in her comments on the learning process of traditional songs in East Suffolk, by Russell (1987) on the key role of the family in the initial training of northern bandsmen and choral society members, and in the Opies' (1985) magisterial exploration of the ethnography, folklore and history of children's singing games, learnt and performed informally in the local contexts of playgrounds, front gardens and cul-de-sacs, back lanes and the grass islands of housing estates.

3.2 Images of Music Teachers

A second strand of research, perhaps better termed a one-person project, is the innovative work on music teachers in eighteenth-century England by Richard Leppert who in *Music and Image* (1988), devotes a chapter to 'Music Education as Praxis'. As evidence he uses images of the teaching of music to upper-class amateurs in England during the period found in paintings, drawings and prints.

Leppert argues that in the eighteenth century, education was a family responsibility, and the self-conscious concern with education centred upon family issues of gender, identity and responsibility: the sexuality of power. The music lesson consequently became a focus for sexuality, and its role in defining the social order. Music was a desirable accomplishment for females because they had time on their hands during adolescence, and this time was controlled by men. Music thus helped to produce an ideologically correct species of woman.

In England, foreigners, particularly Italians, were prized as music teachers. As a result of his analysis of the visual portrayal of music teachers Leppert concludes that they were ambivalent creatures, proud yet deferential, both servants and entrepreneurs, tradesmen and professionals. An abiding concern on behalf of parents was the effect of the music teacher on the female student. The ideal music teacher was a male gender version of the girl's mother: good-tempered, genteel, no vulgarity, no physical constraints, softness of voice.

In an earlier related study, Leppert (1985) concerned himself with the lives of music masters who ministered to the children of the upper class, to indicate the kinds of social conventions at play, and to illuminate the general relation between musical life in eighteenth-century England and the social forces that in part controlled it. Through exploring the lives of well-known music teachers including Burney and Herschel, Leppert concludes that metropolitan teachers were able to live 'a genteel but restricted life', but the job was not easy with its long hours and stiff competition for students. In the provinces such teachers remained poor all their lives, and had to put up with satire, to cope with mediocrity for much of the time dealing with pupils who were proud dabblers expecting to receive compliments.

Leppert's work is innovative in using visual representation as evidence, and in its focus upon the teacher within a historical treatment of an ideology of music anchored in practice. Two recent papers exemplify the potential of this kind of work: Brand and Hunt's (1997) exploration of the images of North American music teachers as represented in movies, and Brehony's (1998) study of representations of schooling in rock and pop music. Future work might lead on from Leppert's view of music education as social praxis by exploring music teachers' lives, their training and careers, reconstructing their classrooms, looking at the intersection of teacher and pupil lives.

3.3 Pedagogical Texts

Pedagogical texts in music can generate powerful insights into music teaching practice, both in terms of social and pedagogical perspectives. Leppert addresses the first of these (1988) and maintains that tutor books in the eighteenth century recreate important information about the taste, state and practice of music among the upper classes, because it was for this group that these texts were written. Potential financial gain and the hope of attracting new students were powerful motivations. Such published tutors guaranteed easy and fast results for 'dabblers'. Leppert infers that these tutors appealed differently to the two genders: for men self-instruction avoided dependence as an adult on a socially inferior music master; for women the issue may have been economic as the result of the husband or father wanting to restrict payment on private lessons. Leppert's conclusion is that the published tutors represented a 'musically dead positivism: how to count, where to place your fingers' (ibid., 69).

The pedagogical nature of such texts has been explored by Kassler (1976) who investigated British instructional materials produced between 1714 and 1830 which were designed to teach young children the first rudiments of music. They contained material pertaining to the mind and body. Corporeal habits were inculcated by various systems of fingering, by instructions for the proper manner of sitting at an instrument, by scale exercises and other mechanical patterns designed to form correctly the position of the hand. Kassler demonstrates that music education during that period was modelled upon language education. The music instruction books taught the musical alphabet. Because the elements were fixed, it was the arrangement of items in the texts that was paramount in order to provide for a clear and distinct exposition. Generally it appears the elements were taught grammatically: first of all the student encountered the different kinds of single elements, then developed them into larger structures like scales, then applied the knowledge of writing the marks and sounds, and finally sang or played the piece.

These published tutors were generally in the form of a catechism, and for young children were presented as question and answer. Kassler traces new developments in the presentation of tutors, particularly in the use of pictures and rhymes. Such materials Kassler regards as historical artefacts which can tell us much about traditional ways of thinking of music and presenting it to beginners.

Musical texts thus provide considerable research opportunities for the educational historian as they communicate a popular and sometimes innovative view of knowledge as well as giving clues about the social class and gender characteristics of their intended audience.

3.4 Music Education, Class and Culture

Music and music education are not esoteric phenomena, but are practices inseparable from the cultures of which they are part (see Humphreys, 1997). The relationships and interactions between music, class and culture and the formation of national and cultural identity through schooling is potentially a rich area of investigation.

In his paper 'Oh Happy English Children', Colls (1976) looked at the titles of songs found in school log books in the 1870s and 1880s, and consequently applied his thesis about education as an agency of social control to North-Eastern mining communities. He argues that marching and patriotic school songs such as 'Oh Happy English Children' or rousing and obedient examples including 'Hark the Whistle Sounding', or sentiments reminiscent of Samuel Smiles, 'Work Hard, help yourselves', were all anthems of missionary intent. Colliery children were paying the price of their fathers' and grandfathers' radical strike action in 1844, out of which, Colls asserts, the coalfield schools were shuffled into existence primarily to break down the patterns of working class self-education which had been so powerful in the strike action. Colls makes a plea for social historians to

> get down from the heady heights of government commissions and company master plans in order to sit with the children ... to know the chalky, dusty experience of boredom that was their education. (Ibid., 98-9)

In such ways Colls' work focuses upon the reconstruction of educational experience, and on education as an agency of cultural reproduction.

Within a different context Adey (1988) set out to show how hymns helped to transmit social class conditioning to children in the late nineteenth and early twentieth centuries by comparing hymn books for charity schools, public schools and board schools. Charity school hymns enjoined work and the profitable use of time, whilst hymnals for orphans inculcated moral attitudes towards the consecration of domestic love and patriotic sentiment. The Board School hymns sold the next world as compensation for the present, whilst submissiveness and 'littleness' were constant themes. In contrast, public school hymns presented a romantic view of childhood, with the watchword 'high manliness'. Adey concludes that God became focused on school, social class and country.

Along similar lines, my own analysis (Cox 1993) of *The National Song Book* (Stanford 1906) related its development to the growth in imperial nationalism and the ideas of Herder and Engel with respect to cultural nationalism and national music. I maintained that music allied to national feeling could produce a unity which stretches across social divisions. This leaves it susceptible to manipulation. It can come to represent the self-interests of a powerful sub-group which has access to manipulative means.

Such considerations of national and cultural identity are the subject of David Allsobrook's book, *Music for Wales* (1992). He examines the image of Wales as 'the Land of Song', and 'the myth of Welsh musicality' and in particular connects his history with the Eisteddfods and the rise of tonic sol-fa on the one hand, and with Welsh folk songs and popular hymnody on the other hand. Allsobrook demonstrates how music education in its widest sense played a crucial part in the development of Welsh culture between 1918 and 1941, by focusing on the work of Walford Davies and the National Council of Music. The strength of the study lies in its placing of institutionalised education side by side with informal and community-based groups within the overarching theme of Welsh culture. Its coverage of school-based education comprises just one chapter, but the whole book can be seen to be concerned with a broader definition of what counts as music education.

Walford Davies believed strongly that music in schools had a crucial part to play in the future musical health of the nation. In contrast, McCarthy's (1999) study of music education in Ireland between 1831 and 1989 puts forward the notion that the strength of music education in Ireland lies outside or on the periphery of the educational system. Her study explores the relationship between musical and cultural development in nineteenth- and twentieth-century Ireland through an investigation of the music transmission process. Underpinning it is the notion of national identity, supported by a view of music as the embodiment of a set of values and beliefs that are inextricably linked to power structures and ideologies.

Ireland provides a valuable site for such an investigation, shaped as it has been by the two political ideologies of colonialism and nationalism. The institutions and communities which contributed to the sense of statehood were frequently associated with musical participation, and this participation in McCarthy's eyes served as both a maker and marker of identity.

The central conflict between traditional Irish musical culture, and the western musical canon in the mid-nineteenth century found its most extreme manifestation within formal schooling, in particular the normal schools, in which the musical diet was based on the Hullah Method of singing at sight. McCarthy views this practice as culturally discontinuous with the experience of the majority of young people the system sought to educate. In contrast were the informal flowerings of Irish musical culture, including temperance movement bands, the Irish Ballad associated with the Young Ireland movement, and traditional music and dance activity.

It becomes clear, as McCarthy concludes, that the strongest and most successful traditions in the transmission of music in Irish culture have developed outside of the formal systems. She identifies three causes of the primary weakness of music education in formal institutions in Ireland: cultural fragmentation produced by colonialism; dependence on a weak economy; the dominant role of competing political ideologies in providing the *raison d'être* for the subject. In comparison, the hope for the future is for an agenda based upon democracy, diversity and inclusiveness.

These studies demonstrate the potential that is to be found in locating music education within the parameters of class and culture. Undoubtedly they mirror some of the advances that have been made within the History of Education since the late 1960s. However, Cohen's (1999) listing of the range of topics tackled by what he calls social historians of education is enlightening: social control and social conflict, urban history, family history, history of women, history of people of colour, history of ethnic and religious minorities, and history 'from the bottom up'. This is not to mention postmodernism, and the construction of what Cohen calls a New Cultural History of Education. Clearly, music education historians have simply scratched the surface, we have much to do. More specifically we badly need more research that will illuminate our understanding of music education's function in fostering a sense of identities that have to be constantly invented, transformed and recovered.

4. Towards a Usable Past for Music Educators

Within the current educational climate in the UK there are constant pleas for research to improve educational practice. In the USA some years ago, Heller and Wilson (1982) insisted that historical research in music education 'must treat questions that contemporary practitioners are concerned about'. More recently Humphreys (1997) has talked of the need for 'outcomes research'.

The danger is that such research becomes myopic and narrow. Ideally the music education historian needs to learn from the insights of the social historian of music (what might be regarded as 'two parallel strands of research overlapping at many points' (Cunningham, 1989, 79)) whilst at the same time engaging with the concerns of teachers and policy makers. It is in facing up to this tension that the future of historical research in music education lies.

How can we do this? How can we escape from Rainbow's and Simpson's rose-tinted view of the educational past into an engagement with the present? McCulloch (1994) is helpful in his argument that establishing the dynamic connections between past, present and future implies an approach to educational history that is present-minded, seeking to provide an understanding of the problems and possibilities of the present. Through such an approach it is possible to construct 'a usable past' (Hansot and Tyack, 1982) in which the problems and limitations of past traditions can be delineated, with the intention of evaluating current educational policies (for a fiercely opposed view, however, see Cohen, 1999, 24-29). In what ways then, can we as researchers in the history of music education create 'a usable past' for music educators?

I will suggest four possibilities. First, an engagement with contemporary policy. Historical studies which confront policy-making decisions create a dialogue between research and practice. Since 1992 music educators in the UK have lived their professional lives within the context of a National Curriculum. Music in the National Curriculum has been the subject of fierce debate, best exemplified by the work of Shepherd and Vulliamy (1994). Although working within an ostensibly sociological framework, they include in their analysis a historical discussion of the 'new sociology of education' which in Britain had its roots in cultural relativism. Central to their argument is that the alienation of children from school music, apparent both in the UK and Canada, was caused by the music curriculum being based upon criteria abstracted from the tradition of the established Western canon. Shepherd and Vulliamy advocate that popular music be introduced according to the criteria associated with those who create and appreciate the music. This historical context provided the basis of their fundamental disagreement with the Conservative government's preliminary proposals for a music national curriculum, which were eventually defeated. What was at stake was the character of English culture. The government wanted in effect a curriculum that reflected white, middle-class musical values, centred upon the western classical tradition. The very different and radical proposals put forward by the Music National Curriculum Committee which reflected more closely the views of music educators with an emphasis upon the pluralist nature of contemporary society, did not represent the image of England that Margaret Thatcher's Conservatives had in mind. Hence, Shepherd and Vulliamy's paper is entitled 'The Struggle for Culture'.

Gammon's (1999) discussion of the English National Curriculum for Music takes the argument further: the new right (or neo-conservatism) and its interventions via the media was crucial in shaping the debate. Gammon contextualises the introduction of the National Curriculum by pointing out that the situation of permanent educational revolution that ensued served a government with a deep distrust of the professions well. Central to the case of the principal new right protagonists, Anthony O'Hear and Roger Scruton, was the belief that music educators wanted to restrict children's experience to pop music, rather than to pass on the cultural heritage which in terms of music was equated with western art music. Gammon's political analysis gives credence to both 'the machinations of a right wing educational mafia' and the British Conservative government's 'desperate attempts to regain credibility with grassroots Tory opinion'.

Since the introduction of the National Curriculum in 1992 there have been all sorts of new and related policy developments to command the attention of the present-minded historian of music education: the revision of the National Curriculum in 2000 (DfEE, 1999); a perceived weakening of the status of music in primary schools in favour of numeracy and literacy; concerns that music might become a voluntary out-of-hours activity for primary age children funded by the National Lottery (Williamson, 1998); the uncertain future of instrumental teaching.

Second, is to develop a curriculum history which disentangles the complexities, constraints and disappointments of curriculum reform. Particularly helpful would be studies of music subject associations and curriculum development projects to provide evidence of conflicting interests, of 'change, contestation and continuity'. There is a paucity of such studies in the UK. However in the USA there is emerging some stimulating work which focuses upon the influence of the powerful Music Educators National Conference (MENC) (see Humphreys and Schmidt, 1998). Recent developments in the teaching of music, including the emphasis upon technology, on World Music, and the growing interest in international links amongst music educators also need situating in a historical context (see Volk, 1998, and McCarthy, 1993, 1995).

Third, investigating teacher and pupil perceptions of teaching and being taught music, so that we can explore the curriculum as it actually was incorporated into school settings. Life history research and oral history provide intriguing ways in to such work. Kevin Thompson's (1999) paper, 'Brass players on playing and teaching' presents an illuminating model for life history work, as it sets out through interviews with three eminent trumpeters, to reflect on issues that have permeated their professional lives including approaches to teaching and learning. In their conversations the experiences of these professionals become vivid and memorable. For example, Philip Jones talks about the nexus of his family influences:

> My maternal grandfather was a trumpet player to start with. He got bored with playing the trumpet in orchestras and became a percussion player ... My father learnt to play the trombone in the army and met up with my mother's father; and my uncle was a trumpet player and spent twenty years playing second trumpet to me in orchestras. (Ibid., 9)

His reflections upon teaching beginners provides a specific view of technique which provides a rich source of information which educational historians will be able to situate historically:

> If you get them first of all to buzz their lips, one they are fascinated that you could do such a thing; two, if you then ask them to put a mouthpiece on to the buzz they discover they can buzz a little higher and a little lower. If you put that into the trumpet they immediately want to do exactly what they did at the beginning which is blow out their cheeks again. But you remind them of the importance of producing a buzz, buzzing into the mouthpiece, and then into the trumpet. The trumpet is only a megaphone. And so the concept is understood and you build your approach to teaching from that. (Ibid., 27)

Finally, Crispian Steele-Perkins addresses the part that teaching has played traditionally in the lives of professional musicians:

> Playing is only a part of one's livelihood. You may have to turn to other forms of employment. A young colleague of mine is managing an off-licence ... Another colleague of mine does two or three months a year as a skiing instructor. When I worked in the Royal Opera House Orchestra, and I had three children to bring up, teaching was a very useful supplement ... I think when we were younger we all expected to do some teaching, but we did it more out of dedication than out of necessity. (Ibid., 40)

The significance of Thompson's paper is that it is intended for experienced brass teachers studying for a diploma, Music Teaching in Professional Practice. Throughout the paper questions are framed that continually challenge these teachers' professional practices related to the oral histories of leading practitioners. In its musical breadth and its focus on practical concerns the paper acts as a pointer for future research.

Fourth, to encourage and enable music teachers to engage with a range of ideas from the past and the present, and so begin to construct a philosophical basis for classroom practice. The work of Stephanie Pitts is notable in this respect. In a paper which addresses the place of music in the contemporary curriculum (Pitts, 2000a) she isolates three principal reasons for teaching music in the twentieth century: music as a desirable cultural influence; music for life and leisure; music for emotional and imaginative development. She asks her readers to relate these ideas to the contemporary perspective.

In her recent book *A Century of Change in Music Education* (2000b) Pitts focuses upon the body of key texts in music education in order to gauge their significance as representatives of the innovations and priorities of past decades, although she adds the proviso that it is difficult to determine the extent of their influence upon teachers. Nevertheless, through their reading of these educators, music teachers are encouraged to ask fundamental questions about the music curriculum, and then to generate their own answers. The strength of such work is that it encourages present-day music teachers to recapture an enthusiasm for music education (Pitts, 1998), thus enabling them to construct 'a story about the present, using items from the past' (Steedman, 1990, 245).

I have attempted in this Afterword to uncover some of the assumptions which have formed the orthodoxy of research in the history of music education, and then to survey a related but fragmented field of work from wider perspectives. The future of research in the history of music education, I suggest, lies in developing the notion of 'an enlarging vision' (McCulloch and Richardson, 2000, 77), through fusing the social and pedagogical traditions of the history of education, and engaging with the real concerns of policy makers, administrators, and practitioners in music classrooms, so that the idea of a usable past becomes a reality. More than anything, it is that notion which this book seeks to develop.

Bibliography

Note: Archival collections cited include the following: BBC Written Archives, Caversham (including School Broadcasting Council report); EMI Music Archives, Hayes; Music Education History Archive, University of Reading (Musical Education of the Under-Twelves/Musical Education up to Thirteen committee papers, Schools Council primary music project papers and correspondence, tapes and transcripts of interviews with secondary school music teachers and student teachers, Arnold Bentley interview notes, Cox correspondence, Rainbow correspondence); National Sound Archive, London (programme recordings from the BBC Sound Archives); Public Record Office, Kew (Schools Council Music Committee papers, Schools Council secondary school music project consultative committee papers).

Adair, Y. (1952) *Music through the Percussion Band: A comprehensive scheme of work from the earliest stages, with games and exercises for playing, listening, reading and conducting.* London: Boosey and Co.

Adey, L. (1988) *Class and Idol in the English Hymn.* Vancouver: University of British Columbia.

Aldrich, R. (2000) 'A contested and changing terrain: history of education in the twenty-first century', in Crook, D. and Aldrich, R. (eds.), *History of Education for the Twenty-First Century.* London: University of London Institute of Education. Bedford Way Papers.

Allsobrook, D.I. (1990) 'Two figures in the landscape of Welsh music education: W.H. Hadow and Walford Davies', *History of Education* 19 (3), pp. 219-34.

Allsobrook, D.I. (1992) *Music for Wales: Walford Davies and the National Music Council 1918-1941.* Cardiff: University of Wales.

Ball, S.J. and Goodson, I.F. (eds.) (1985) *Teachers' Lives and Careers.* London: The Falmer Press.

Banfield, S. (1985) *Sensibility and English Song: Critical Studies of the Early Twentieth Century.* Cambridge: Cambridge University Press.

Barber, M. (1996) *Beyond the Numbers Game: Arguments for an Educational Revolution.* London: Victor Gollancz.

Bennet, C. (1985) 'Paints, Pots or Promotion: Art Teachers' Attitudes towards Their Careers', Ball, S.J. and Goodson, I.F. (eds.), *Teachers' Lives and Careers.* London: The Falmer Press.

Bentley, A. (n.d.) University of Reading/Schools Council Research and Development Project on 'Music Education of Young Children'. Typescript. Music Education History Archive, University of Reading.

Bentley, A. (1998) Interview with Gordon Cox, 15 June. Notes deposited in the Music Education History Archive, University of Reading.

Blocksidge, K. (1934) *Percussion and Pipe Bands.* Foreword by Margaret James. London: Augener.

Blocksidge, K. (1957) *Making Musical Apparatus and Instruments for use in Nursery and Infant Schools.* London: Nursery School Association.

Bloomfield, A. (2001) 'The quickening of the national spirit: Cecil Sharp and the pioneers of the folk-dance revival in English state schools (1900-1926)', *History of Education* 30 (1), pp. 59-75.

Board of Education (1926) *Report of the Consultative Committee on the Education of the Adolescent.* London: HMSO.

Board of Education (1933) *Recent Developments in School Music.* London: HMSO. Educational Pamphlets No. 95.

Board of Education (1937) *Handbook of Suggestions for Teachers.* London: HMSO.

Bottum, J. (2000) 'Drowning in Music', *New Statesman,* 7 August.

Bouij, C. (1999) 'Swedish Music Teachers in Training and Professional Life', *International Journal of Music Education,* 32, pp. 24-32.

The Bow-Craft Guild (1948) *A comprehensive and approved scheme for the development of School Orchestras.* London: J. Williams. 3rd edition.

Boyle, J.D. (1979) 'Review of *Time for Music*', *Psychology of Music* 7 (2), pp. 41-7.

Brand, M. and Hunt, K. (1997) 'The Celluloid Music Teacher: An Examination of Cinematic Portrayals of Music Teaching and Music Education in Films', in Rideout, R. (ed.), *On the Sociology of Music Education.* Norman, OK: The University of Oklahoma School of Music.

Brehony, K.J. (1998) '"I used to get mad at my school": Representations of schooling in rock and pop music', *British Journal of Sociology of Education* 19 (1), pp. 113-34.

Briggs, A. (1965) *The History of Broadcasting in the United Kingdom: Vol. 2 The Golden Age of Wireless.* London: Oxford University Press.

Briggs, A. (1972) 'The Study of the History of Education', *History of Education* 1, pp. 5-22.

British Broadcasting Corporation (BBC) (n.d.) *Junior Music Lesson.* Ref. 727. BBC Sound Archive.

BBC (1934) *Broadcasts to Schools. Music Lessons. Term II.* London: BBC.

BBC (1934-1935) *Music Handbook for Teachers.* London: BBC.

BBC (1937) *BBC Annual.* London: BBC.

BBC (1944) *Music and Movement* broadcast, 6 November. BBC Sound Archive.

BBC (1949) *BBC Handbook.* London: BBC.

BBC (1962) *Scottish Life and Letters* broadcast, Herbert Wiseman, 31 December. BBC Sound Archive LP28639.

BBC Written Archives (1929-1936) Advisory Committee, School Broadcasting Council, Music Programme Sub-Committee Minute Book. R6/130/1

BBC Written Archives (1934) Ann Driver File 1a.

BBC Written Archives (1936-1946) Education General: Schools Programmes - Music File 1. R6/130/2.

BBC Written Archives (1939-1941) Sir Walford Davies File 5b.

Brown, J.H. (1938) *Instrumental Music in Schools.* London: Pitman.

Bullough, R.V Jnr., Knowles, J.G. and Crow, N.A. (1991) *Emerging as a Teacher.* London: Routledge.

Bunting, R. (1976) *The Common Language of Music: A Discussion Paper.* York: University of York Department of Music. Music in the Secondary School Curriculum Working Paper 6.

Button, S. (1989) 'Ferdinand Pelzer: an Introduction to a Neglected Achievement', *British Journal of Music Education* 6, 1989, pp. 241-50.

Cain, J. and Wright, B. (1994) *In a Class of its own ... BBC Education 1924-1994.* London: BBC.

Central Advisory Council for Education (CACE) (1963) *Half Our Future.* (The Newsom Report). London: HMSO.

Central Advisory Council for Education (CACE) (1967) *Children and their Primary Schools.* (The Plowden Report). London: HMSO.

Chanan, M. (1995) *Repeated Takes: A Short History of Recording and its Effects on Music.* London: Verso.

Cohen, S. (1999) *Challenging Orthodoxies: Towards a New Cultural History of Education.* New York: Peter Lang.

Coll, H. (1998) 'Where have all the Teachers gone?', *Yes,* 28, p. 18.

Colles, H.C. (1942) *Walford Davies: A Biography.* London: Oxford University Press.

Colls, R. (1976) '"Oh Happy English Children": Coal, Class and Education in the North-East', *Past and Present* 73, pp. 75-99.

Connell, R.W. (1985) *Teachers' Work.* Sydney: George Allen and Unwin.

County of Kent (1927) *Educational Broadcasting: Report of a Special Investigation in the County of Kent during the year 1927.* Dunfermline: The Carnegie UK Trustees.

Cox, C.B. and Dyson, A.E. (eds.) (1971) *The Black Papers on Education.* London: Davis-Poynter.

Cox Correspondence (2000) Letter from Jack Dobbs, 7 September, Music Education History Archive, University of Reading.

Cox, G. (1993) *A History of Music Education in England 1872-1928.* Aldershot: Scolar Press.

Cox, G. (1996) 'School music broadcasts and the BBC 1924-47', *History of Education* 25 (4), pp. 363-71.

Cox, G. (1998) 'Adult Singing Schools in Reading 1842-1845', *Berkshire Old and New* 15, pp. 13-21.

Cox, G. (1999) 'Towards a Usable Past for Music Educators', *History of Education* 28 (4), pp. 449-58.

Cunningham, P. (1988) *Curriculum Change in the Primary School Since 1945: Dissemination of the Progressive Ideal.* London: Falmer.

Cunningham, P. (1989) 'Educational History and Educational Change: The Past Decade of English Historiography', *History of Education Quarterly* 29 (1), pp. 77-94.

Dale, R.R. (1941) 'Music Broadcasts for Schools', *Music in Schools*, March-April, pp. 197-8.

Daunt, S. (1976) *Music, School and Young People: A Report for the Schools Council Project: Music in the Secondary School Curriculum.* York: University of York Department of Music. Music in the Secondary School Curriculum Working Paper 3.

Davies, H.W. (1915a) *Thirty-eight Songs for Camp Concerts.* London: Sidney Riordan.

Davies, H.W. (1915b) *Thirty Songs Old and New for Use in War-time.* London: Sidney Riordan.

Davies, H.W. (1915c) *The Fellowship Song Book.* London: J. Curwen and Headley Bros.

Davies, H.W. (1916) *Choruses, Songs and Hymn Tunes.* YMCA with the Expeditionary Force in France. London: J. Curwen.

Davies, H.W. (1922) *Melody Lectures.* 9 double-sided 12" 78 rpm records. His Master's Voice (HMV) C1063-1071.

Davies, H.W. (1926) *Melody Book No. 1.* London: BBC.

Davies, H.W. (1929a) *Twelve Talks on Melody: Listener's Guide Book.* London: The Gramophone Company.

Davies, H.W. (1929b) *Twelve Talks on Melody.* 9 double-sided 12" 78 rpm records. HMV C1759-1767.

Davies, H.W. (1931) *The New Fellowship Song Book.* London: Novello.

Davies, H.W. (1933a) *First Steps in Music: An Introduction to the Study and Teaching of Music.* London: MacMillan.

Davies, H.W. (1933b) *A Four Years' Course for Music with Lesson Notes: for the use of Music Teachers in Primary and Preparatory Schools.* London: MacMillan.

Davies, H.W. (1935) *The Pursuit of Music.* London: Nelson.

Debble, J. (1992) *C. Hubert Parry: His Life and Music.* Oxford: Clarendon Press.

Dent, H.C. (1977) *The Training of Teachers in England and Wales 1800-1975.* London: Hodder and Stoughton.

Department for Education (DfE) (1992) *Initial Teacher Training (secondary phase).* Circular 9/92. London: DfE.

Department for Education and Employment (DfEE), Qualifications and Curriculum Authority (QCA) (1999) *The National Curriculum for England: Music.* London: DfEE/QCA.

Department of Education and Science (DES) (1970) *Creative Music in Schools.* Reports on Education Number 63. London: HMSO.

DES (1985) *Music 5-16*. London: HMSO.

DES (1989) *Initial Teacher Training: Approval of Course*. Circular 24/89. London: DES.

Dobbs, J. (1976) 'Emile Jaques-Dalcroze', in Simpson, K. (ed.), *Some Great Music Educators: A Collection of Essays*. Borough Green: Novello.

Dobbs, J.P.B. and Firth, W. (1959) *Oxford School Music Books: Infant Book*. London: Oxford University Press.

Driver, A. (1936) *Music and Movement*. London: Oxford University Press.

Dunn, G. (1980) *The Fellowship of Song: Popular Singing Traditions in East Suffolk*. London: Croom Helm.

EMI Music Archives (1929) Correspondence: Sir Walford Davies and Mr Lack.

Evans, J. and McNaught, W.G. (1903) *The School Music Teacher: A Guide to the Teaching of Singing in Schools by Tonic Sol-fa Notation and Staff Notation*. London: J. Curwen. Ninth Edition.

Everitt, A. (1997) *Joining In: An Investigation into Participatory Music*. London: Calouste Gulbenkian Foundation.

Fawcett, B. (1982) *The Gloucester Evaluation of Time for Music: Second Report*. Reading: University of Reading/Schools Council Project, 'Music Education of Young Children'.

Finkelstein, B. (1989) *Governing the Young: Teacher Behavior in Popular Primary Schools in Nineteenth-century United States*. New York: Falmer.

Finnegan, R. (1989) *The Hidden Musicians: Music-Making in an English Town*. Cambridge: Cambridge University Press.

Fiske, R. and Dobbs, J.P.B. (1954-1961) *Oxford School Music Books: Junior Series*. Books 1-4. London: Oxford University Press.

Franklin, B. (1999) 'The state of curriculum history', *History of Education* 28(4), pp. 459-76.

Froebel, F. (1907) *Mother's Songs, Games and Stories. Frobel's 'Mutter und Kose Lieder'*. Rendered in English by F. and E. Lord. London: William Rice. First published by Froebel 1843.

Gammon, V. (1996) 'What is wrong with school music? - a response to Malcolm Ross', *British Journal of Music Education* 13, pp. 101-22.

Gammon, V. (1999) 'Cultural Politics of the English National Curriculum', *Journal of Educational Administration and History* 31(2), pp. 130-47.

Gammon, V. and Gammon, S. (2000) 'The Musical Revolution of the Mid-Nineteenth Century: From "Repeat and Twiddle" to "Precision and Snap"', in Herbert, T. (ed.), *The British Brass Band: A Musical and Social History*. Oxford: Oxford University Press.

Goodson, I.F. (ed.) (1985) *Social Histories of the Secondary Curriculum: Subjects for Study*. London: Falmer.

Goodson, I.F. (1988) *The Making of Curriculum: Collected Essays*. London: The Falmer Press.

Goodson, I.F. (1993) *School Subjects and Curriculum Change: Studies in Curriculum History*. London: The Falmer Press. Third edition.

Goodson, I.F. (1994) *Studying Curriculum*. Buckingham: Open University.

Goodson, I.F. with Anstead, C.J. and Mangan, J.M. (1998) *Subject Knowledge: Readings for the Study of School Subjects*. London: The Falmer Press.

Goodson, I.F. with Mangan, J.M. (1998) 'Subject Cultures and the Introduction of Classroom Computers', in I.F. Goodson *et al.*, *Subject Knowledge*.

Goodson, I.F. and Marsh, C.J. (1996) *Studying School Subjects: A Guide*. London: The Falmer Press.

Goodson, I.F. and Walker, R. (1988) 'Putting Life into Educational Research', in Sherman, R.R. and Webb, R.B. (eds.), *Qualitative Research in Education: Focus and Methods*. London: The Falmer Press.

Gordon, P. (1989) 'The Schools Council and Curriculum Developments in Secondary Education', in Lowe, R. (ed.), *The Changing Secondary School*. London: Falmer.

Gordon, P., Aldrich, R. and Dean, D. (1991) *Education and Policy in England in the Twentieth Century.* London: Woburn Press.

Gordon, P. and Szreter, R. (eds.) (1989) *History of Education: The Making of a Discipline.* London: Woburn Press.

Green, K. (2000) 'Book Review Essay: Understanding Physical Education Teachers' Lives, "Philosophies" and "Practices"', *European Journal of Physical Education* 5, pp. 259-71.

Green, L. (1992) 'The Position of Music in the Technical and Vocational Education Initiative (TVEI): a Critical Appraisal', *British Journal of Music Education* 9 (2), pp. 152-62.

Griffiths, P. (1977) 'The York Project', *Music in Education* 41, pp. 74-7.

Hancox, G.R. (1988) 'The Dissemination of Innovation with special reference to the Schools Council Project "Music in the Secondary School Curriculum"', unpublished MEd thesis, University of Wales.

Hansot, E. and Tyack, D. (1982) 'A Usable Past: Using History in Educational Policy', in Lieberman, A. and McLaughlin, M.W. (eds.), *Policy Making in Education: Eighty-first Yearbook of the National Society for the Study of Education.* Part One. Chicago: NSSE.

Hargreaves, A. (1994) *Changing Teachers, Changing Times: teachers' work and culture in the post-modern age.* London: Cassell.

Hargreaves, A. (1997) 'Realities of teaching', in Saha, L.J. (ed.), *International Encyclopaedia of the Sociology of Education.* Oxford: Pergamon.

Heerwart, E. (1877) *Music for the Kindergarten: Hymns, Songs, and Games for use in the Kindergarten, the Family, and the Infant School.* London: Boosey and Co. Eighth Edition.

Heller, G.N. and Wilson, B.D. (1982) 'Historical Research in Music Education: a Prolegomena', *Bulletin of the Council of Research in Music Education* 69, pp. 1-20.

Helsby, G. and McCulloch, G. (1996) 'Teacher Professionalism and Curriculum Control', in Goodson, I. and Hargreaves, A. (eds.), *Teachers' Professional Lives.* London: Falmer.

Hickson, W.E. (1836) *The Singing Master.* London: E. Wilson and J. Hart.

Hobsbawm, E. and Ranger, T. (eds.) (1983) *The Invention of Tradition.* Cambridge: Cambridge University Press.

Hodge, G.M., Jupp, J.J. and Taylor A.J. (1994) 'Work stress, distress and burnout in music and mathematics teachers', *British Journal of Educational Psychology* 64, pp. 65-76.

Horton, J. (1947) 'Music', in Palmer, R. (ed.), *School Broadcasting in Britain.* London: BBC.

Horton, J. (1972) *British Primary Schools Today: Music.* London: MacMillan.

Horton, J. (1976) 'Carl Orff', in Simpson, K. (ed.), *Some Great Music Educators: A Collection of Essays.* Borough Green: Novello.

Houghton, W. (1951) *Guide to the Teaching of Class Music for the Under-eights.* London: Augener.

Houghton, W. (1957) *The study and practice of Rhythmic Movement and Music: A Sequence of Simple Exercises in the Dalcroze Method.* London: Augener.

Huberman, M. (1993) *The Lives of Teachers.* Trans by J. Neufeld. London: Cassell.

Humphreys, J.T. (1997) 'Expanding the Horizons of Music Education History and Sociology', *The Quarterly Journal of Music Teaching and Learning* VII, pp. 5-19.

Humphreys, J.T. and Schmidt, C. (1998) 'Membership of the Music Educators National Conference from 1912-1938: A demographic and economic analysis', *Bulletin of the Council for Research in Music Education* 137, pp. 16-31.

Hunt, E.B. (1922) *Spirit and Music.* London: Kegan Paul, Trench, Trubner and Co; J. Curwen and Sons.

James, M. (1932) *The Pipers' Guild Handbook.* London: J.B. Cramer.

Jaques-Dalcroze, E. (1967) *Rhythm Music and Education.* Woking: The Dalcroze Society. First published 1921.

Jenkins, E.W. and Swinnerton, B.J. (1996) 'The School Nature Study Union 1903-94', *History of Education* 25, pp. 181-98.

Judge, H., Lemosse, M., Paine, L. and Sedlak, M. (1994) *The University and the Teachers: France, the United States, England.* Wallingford: Triangle Books.

Kassler, J.C. (1976) 'Music Made Easy to Infant Capacity 1714-1830: Some Facets of British Music Education', *Studies in Music* 10, pp. 67-78.

Kendell, I. (1974) 'The New Phase', *Music Teacher*, 11 July.

Kendell, I. (1976) 'If you can teach reading, you can teach music', *Dialogue* 22, Spring, pp. 8-9.

Kendell, I. (1977) 'The Role of Literacy in the School Music', in Burnett, M. (ed.), *Music Education Review: A Handbook for Music Teachers.* Vol.1. London: Chappell.

Kendell, I. (1979) 'A Study of the Learning Processes of Young Children in Music by means of the Development of a Structured Programme to Teach Musical Literacy'. Unpublished PhD dissertation, University of Reading.

Kendell, I. (1984) 'The Primary Music Curriculum - Some Ways Ahead', *Psychology of Music* 12 (2), pp. 126-30.

Kendell, I.P., Allin, S. and Walkley, C. (1976-1978) *Time for Music.* Teachers' Support Book, 3-5 Stage, Infant Stage, Link Stage, Junior 1 Stage, Junior 2 Stage. Leeds: E.J. Arnold.

Kenyon, N. (1981) *The BBC Symphony Orchestra: The First Fifty Years.* London: BBC.

King, G. (1998) 'Exemplary Music Educator: A Case Study', *Bulletin of the Council for Research in Music Education* 137, pp. 57-72.

Kliebard, H.M. (1995) *The Struggle for the American Curriculum 1893-1958.* Second Edition. London: Routledge.

Knight, P. (1996) 'Subject Associations: the cases of secondary phase geography and home economics, 1976-94', *History of Education* 25, pp. 269-84.

Knowles, J.G. (1992) 'Models for understanding pre-service and beginning teachers' biographies: Illustrations from case studies', in Goodson, I.F. (ed.), *Studying Teachers' Lives.* London: Routledge.

Lawrence, I. (1985) 'Aspects of music education in the late eighteenth century', *History of Education* 14 (1), pp. 21-34.

Leppert, R. (1985) 'Music Teachers of Upper-Class Amateur Musicians in Eighteenth Century England', in Atlas, A.W. (ed.), *Music in the Classic Period: Essays in Honor of Barry S. Brook.* New York: Pendragon.

Leppert, R. (1988) *Music and Image: Domesticity, ideology and socio-cultural formation in Eighteenth Century England.* Cambridge: Cambridge University Press.

Lowe, R. (1988) *Education in the Post-War Years: A Social History.* London: Routledge.

Maconie, R. (1977) 'Structured Ignorance', *Times Educational Supplement*, 1 April.

MacPherson, S. and Read, E. (1912) *Aural Culture Based upon Musical Appreciation.* London: Joseph Williams.

Madsen, C. (ed.) (2000) *Vision 2020: The Housewright Symposium on the Future of Music Education.* Reston, VA: MENC.

Mark, D. (1999) 'The music teacher's dilemma - musician or teacher?', *International Journal of Music Education* 32, pp. 3-23.

Marsden, W.E. (1991) *Educating the Respectable: A Study of the Fleet Road Board School, Hampstead 1879-1903.* London: Woburn Press.

McCarthy, M. (1993) 'The Birth of Internationalism in Music Education 1899-1938', *International Journal of Music Education* 21, pp. 3-9.

McCarthy, M. (1995) 'Canticle to Hope: Widening Horizons in International Music Education 1939-1953', *International Journal of Music Education* 25, pp. 32-49.

McCarthy, M. (1999) *Passing It On: The Transmission of Music in Irish Culture.* Cork: University of Cork.

McCulloch, G. (1994) *Educational Reconstruction: The 1944 Education Act and the Twenty-first Century.* London: Woburn Press.

McCulloch, G. and Richardson, W. (eds.) (2000) *Historical Research in Educational Settings.* Buckingham: Open University.

MEUT *Bulletin* (1949-1981).

Mills, J. (1997) 'A Comparison of the Quality of Class Music Teaching in Primary and Secondary Schools in England', *Bulletin of the Council for Research in Music Education* 133, pp. 72-6.

Ministry of Education (1956, 1969) *Music in Schools.* London: HMSO.

Music Education Council (MEC) (1998) *The Fourth 'R': the case for music in the school curriculum.* West Horsley: The Campaign for Music in the Curriculum.

Music Education History Archive (1995-1997) Tapes and Transcripts of Interviews with secondary school music teachers, and student teachers. University of Reading.

Music in Education (1947-50, 1973-74).

Music in Schools (March-April 1938, March-April 1940, January-February 1941).

Music Teacher (1923-24, 1948-49, 1968, 1973-74, 1998-99).

Musical Education of the Under-Twelves/ Musical Education Up to Thirteeen (MEUT) (1949-1984) Minutes. Music Education History Archive, University of Reading.

Musical Times (1941).

Nettel, R. (1944) *Music in the Five Towns: A Study of the Social Influence of Music in an Industrial District.* London: Oxford University Press.

News Sheet. (1974-1979) Schools Council Project: 'Music in the Secondary School Curriculum'.

North West Regional Curriculum Development Project (NWRCDP) (1974) *Creative Music Making and the Young School Leaver.* London: Blackie.

Odam, G. (2000) 'Teaching composing in secondary schools: the creative dream', *British Journal of Music Education* 17 (2), pp. 109-28.

Opie, I. and P. (1985) *The Singing Game.* Oxford: Oxford University Press.

Orff, C. (1978) *The Schulwerk.* New York: Schott. Volume 3 of *Carl Orff/Documentation, His Life and Work.* Translated by Margaret Murray.

Paynter, J. (1967) 'Music in a Liberal Education: Learning from the Present', *Music in Education* 31, pp. 22-6.

Paynter, J. (1982) *Music in the Secondary School Curriculum.* Cambridge: Cambridge University Press.

Paynter, J. and Aston, P. (1970) *Sound and Silence: Classroom Projects in Creative Music.* Cambridge: Cambridge University Press.

Pickard, P.M. (1970) *Psychology of developing children.* London: Longman.

Pitts, S. (1998) 'Recapturing an Enthusiasm for Music Education from Innovatory Writings', *British Journal of Music Education* 15 (1), pp. 25-36.

Pitts, S. (2000a) 'Reasons to teach music: establishing a place in the contemporary curriculum', *British Journal of Music Education* 17 (1), pp. 33-42.

Pitts, S. (2000b) *A Century of Change in Music Education: Historical Perspectives on Contemporary Practice in British Secondary School Music.* Aldershot: Ashgate.

Plaskow, M. (ed.) (1985) *Life and Death of the Schools Council.* London: Falmer.

Pollard, H.M. (1956) *Pioneers of Popular Education 1760-1850.* London: John Murray

Poulsen, E. and McLeod, F. (1999) *Survey: The Views of Second-Year Music Students in England and Wales, and Practising Teachers, on School Music Teaching as a Career.* London: Incorporated Society of Musicians.

Rainbow, B. (1967) *The Land without Music: Musical Education in England 1800-1860 and Its Continental Antecedents.* London: Novello.

Rainbow, B. (1980) *John Curwen: A Short Critical Biography.* Borough Green: Novello.

Rainbow, B. (1985) *Onward from Butler: School Music 1945-1985.* London: The Curwen Institute.

Rainbow, B. (1989) *Music in Educational Thought and Practice: A Survey from 800 BC.* Aberystwyth: Boethius.

Rainbow, B. (1990) *Bernarr Rainbow: A List of Books on Music in Education.* Aberystwyth: Boethius.

Rainbow, B. (1993) 'That Great Dust-Heap Called "History"', *International Journal of Music Education* 20, pp. 9-17.

Rainbow Correspondence (1970) Letter to Bernarr Rainbow from Kathleen Blocksidge, 1 March 1970. Music Education History Archive, University of Reading.

Read, H. (1943) *Education Through Art.* London: Faber and Faber.

Richardson, W. (1999) 'Historians and educationists: the history of education as a field of study in post-war England, Part II: 1972-96', *History of Education* 28 (2), pp. 109-141.

Robertson, A. (1961) *More than Music.* London: Collins.

Rose, J. (1984) *The Edwardian Temperament 1895-1919.* Athens, Ohio: Ohio University Press.

Ross, M. (1995) 'What's Wrong with School Music?', *British Journal of Music Education* 12 (3), pp. 185-201.

Royal Society of Arts (1995) *Guaranteeing an Entitlement to the Arts in Schools.* London: RSA.

Royal Society of Arts (1998) *The Disappearing Arts? The current state of the arts in initial teacher training and professional development.* London: Calouste Gulbenkian Foundation.

Russell, D. (1987) *Popular Music in England 1840-1914: A Social History.* Manchester: Manchester University Press.

Russell, D. (1993) 'The "social history" of popular music: a label without a cause?', *Popular Music* 12 (2), pp. 130-54.

Russell-Smith, G. (1976) 'Zoltan Kodály', in Simpson, K. (ed.), *Some Great Music Educators: A Collection of Essays.* Borough Green: Novello.

Salaman, W. (1988) 'Personalities in World Music Education No 7- John Paynter', *International Journal of Music Education* 12, pp. 28-32.

Sandor, F. (1969) *Musical Education in Hungary.* London: Boosey and Hawkes.

Scannell, P. and Cardiff, D. (1991) *A Social History of British Broadcasting. Vol.1: Serving the Nation, 1922-1939.* Oxford: Blackwell.

Schmidt, M. (1998) 'Defining "Good" Music Teaching: Four Student Teachers' Beliefs and Practices', *Bulletin of the Council for Research in Music Education* 138, pp. 19-46.

Scholes, P. (1935) *Music, the child and the masterpiece: A Comprehensive Handbook of aims and methods in all that is usually called 'Musical Appreciation'.* London: Oxford University Press.

Scholes, P. (1947) *The Mirror of Music 1844-1944: A Century of Musical Life in Britain as Reflected in the Pages of the Musical Times.* London: Novello and Oxford University Press.

School Broadcasting Council (c1953) *Music in the Junior School: Draft Report.* BBC Written Archives R16/318.

School Music Review (1923-24-25).

Schools Council (n.d.) 'Basic Music'. Unpublished ms. Music Education History Archive, University of Reading.

Schools Council (1967) Music Committee Membership and Terms of Reference. File EJ2/38, Public Record Office (PRO).

Schools Council (1967-78) Music Committee Minutes. File EJ1/156, Public Record Office (PRO).

Schools Council (1968) *Enquiry One: Young School Leavers.* London: HMSO.

Schools Council (1971) *Music and the Young School Leaver: Problems and Opportunities.* London: Evans/Methuen Educational. Working Paper 35.

Schools Council (1971-1978) 'Music Education of Young Children', Consultative Committee files (MEYCCC). Music Education History Archive, University of Reading.

Schools Council (1972a) *Music Education of Young Children.* Project Profile (CR 03 02). London: HMSO.

Schools Council (1972b) *Music and Integrated Studies in the Secondary School.* London: Schools Council. A bulletin prepared by a working party of the Schools Council Music Committee.

Schools Council Working Paper (1973) *A Survey of the Present State of Music in Primary Schools.* Reading: Schools Council/University of Reading.

Schools Council (1973-1977) Correspondence. Music Education History Archive, University of Reading.

Schools Council (1974-80) 'Music in the Secondary School Curriculum', Consultative Committee minutes. File EJ1/51, Public Record Office (PRO).

Schools Council (1975) *Arts and the Adolescent: a curriculum study from the Schools Council's Arts and the Adolescent Project based at the University of Exeter Institute of Education (1968-1972).* London: Evans/Methuen Educational.

Schools' Music Association (1961) *Report on Music in Primary Schools.* Bromley: Schools' Music Association.

Shaw, G. (1932) 'Developments and Explorations in Musical Education', *Music Teacher,* March, pp. 127-9.

Shepherd, J. and Vulliamy, G. (1994) 'The Struggle for Culture: a sociological case study of the development of a national music curriculum', *British Journal of Sociology of Education* 15, pp. 27-40.

Sikes, P.J. (1987) 'A Kind of Oasis: Art Rooms and Art Teachers in Secondary Schools', in Tickle, L. (ed.), *The Arts in Education: Some Research Studies.* London: Croom Helm.

Sikes, P.J., Measor, L. and Woods, P. (1985) *Teacher Careers: Crises and Continuities.* London: The Falmer Press.

Silver, H. (1983) *Education as History: Interpreting nineteenth- and twentieth-century education.* London: MacMillan.

Simon, B. (1974) *The Politics of Educational Reform 1920-1940.* London: Lawrence and Wishart.

Simon, B. (1991) *Education and the Social Order 1940-1990.* London: Lawrence and Wishart.

Simpson, K. (ed.) (1976) *Some Great Music Educators: A Collection of Essays.* Borough Green: Novello.

Smith, P. (1950) 'Music in Education Since the 1944 Act', *Music in Education,* January-February, pp. 166-7.

Somerville, M. (1947) 'How School Broadcasting Grew Up', in Palmer, R. (ed.), *School Broadcasting in Britain.* London: BBC.

Southcott, J. (1992) 'The Percussion Band - Mere Noise or Music?', *British Journal of Music Education* 9 (2), pp. 111-22.

Spearman, C.E. (2000) 'How will Societal and Technological Changes Affect the Teaching of Music?', in Madsen, C. (ed.), *Vision 2020: The Housewright Symposium on the Future of Music Education.* Reston, Va: MENC.

Spencer, P. (1974) *The Influence of Pop on Creative Music in the Classroom.* York: University of York Department of Music. Music in the Secondary School Curriculum Working Paper 1.

Standing Conference of Music Committees (1954) *The Training of Music Teachers.* London: Standing Conference of Music Committees.

Stanford, C.V. (ed.) (1906) *The National Song Book.* London: Boosey.

Steedman, C. (1990) *Childhood Culture and Class: Margaret McMillan 1860-1931.* London: Virago.

Stone, A.L. (1949) *Story of a School: A headmaster's experiences with children aged seven to eleven.* London: HMSO. Ministry of Education Pamphlet Number Fourteen.

Stradling, R. and Hughes, M. (1993) *The English Musical Renaissance: Construction and Deconstruction.* London: Routledge.

Swanwick, K. (1975) 'Music in Schools Conference', *Music Teacher*, May, pp. 9-10.

Swanwick, K. (1977) 'Belief and Action in Music Education', in Burnett, M. (ed.), *Music Education Review: A Handbook for Music Teachers.* Vol.1. London: Chappell.

Swanwick, K. (1979) *A Basis for Music Education.* Windsor: NFER/Nelson.

Swanwick, K. (1997) 'False Notes', *Times Educational Supplement*, November 14.

Swanwick, K. (1999) *Teaching Music Musically.* London: Routledge.

Taylor, D. (1979) *Music Now: A Guide to Recent Developments and Current Opportunities in Music Education.* Milton Keynes: Open University.

Thackray, R. (1969) 'Rhythmic abilities and their measurement'. Unpublished PhD thesis, University of Reading.

Thackray, R. (1974) *Some Research Projects in Music Education. Interim Report.* University of Reading/Schools Council.

Theberge, P. (1993) 'Random Access: Music technology, post-modernism', in Miller, S. (ed.), *The Last Post: Music after Modernism.* Manchester: Manchester University Press.

Thompson, K. (1999) 'Brass players on playing and teaching', in Cox, G. and Thompson, K. (eds.), *Music Teaching in Professional Practice Module 3: Brass.* Reading: International Centre for Research in Music Education, University of Reading.

Times Educational Supplement (1998-99).

Tingey, N. (1980) *Emile Jaques-Dalcroze: A Record of the London School of Dalcroze Eurhythmics and its Graduates at Home and Overseas.* London: Dalcroze Teachers' Union.

Venables, L.C. (n.d.) *The School Teacher's Music Guide.* London: J. Curwen. Sixth Edition.

The Voice (1922) 'Education Notes: Melody Lecture Records', VI (8), pp. 3-4.

Volk, T. (1998) *Music, Education and Multiculturalism: Foundations and Principles.* New York: Oxford University Press.

Wells, H.G. (1921) *The Salvaging of Civilisation.* London: Cassell.

Williamson, N. (1998) 'Lottery to fund music lessons', *Times Educational Supplement*, 3 March.

Wiseman, H. (1967) *The Singing Class.* Oxford: Pergamon.

Witkin, R. (1974) *The Intelligence of Feeling.* London: Heinemann.

Wolfe, K.M. (1984) *The Churches and the British Broadcasting Corporation 1922-1956.* London: SCM Press.

Woodham-Smith, P. (1952) 'History of the Froebel Movement in England', in Lawrence, E. (ed.), *Friedrich Froebel and English Education.* London: University of London Press. Chapter 2.

Woods, P. (1984) 'Teacher, self and curriculum', in Goodson, I.F. and Ball, S.J. (eds.), *Defining the Curriculum: Histories and Ethnographies.* London: Falmer.

Yarborough, C. (2000) 'What should be the relationship between schools and other sources of music learning?', in Madsen, C. (ed.), *Vision 2020: The Housewright Symposium on the Future of Music Education.* Reston, Va: MENC.

Zagni, F. (1989) *'Uncle Ernie'- the biography of Ernest Read, pioneer of youth orchestras and musical education.* London: Thames Publishing.

Index